THIRD EDITION

RESUMES FOR

COLLEGE STUDENTS AND RECENT GRADUATES

Includes Sample Cover Letters

The Editors of VGM Career Books

VGM Career Books

New York   Chicago   San Francisco   Lisbon   London   Madrid   Mexico City
Milan   New Delhi   San Juan   Seoul   Singapore   Sydney   Toronto

Library of Congress Cataloging-in-Publication Data

Resumes for college students and recent graduates / the editors of VGM Career Books.—3rd ed.
p.   cm. — (VGM professional resumes series)
ISBN 0-07-143737-1 (pbk. : alk. paper)
1. Resumes (Employment)   2. College graduates—Employment.   3. College students—Employment.   I. VGM Career Books (Firm)   II. Series.

HF5383.R434   2004
650.14′2—dc22   2004040263

3 4 5 6 7 8 9 0   QPD/QPD   3 2 1 0 9 8 7 6

ISBN 0-07-143737-1

McGraw-Hill books are available at special quantity discounts to use as premiums and sales promotions, or for use in corporate training programs. For more information, please write to the Director of Special Sales, Professional Publishing, McGraw-Hill, Two Penn Plaza, New York, NY 10121-2298. Or contact your local bookstore.

This book is printed on acid-free paper.

Contents

Introduction

Your resume is a piece of paper (or an electronic document) that serves to introduce you to the people who will eventually hire you. To write a thoughtful resume, you must thoroughly assess your personality, your accomplishments, and the skills you have acquired. The act of composing and submitting a resume also requires you to carefully consider the company or individual that might hire you. What are they looking for, and how can you meet their needs? This book shows you how to organize your personal information and experience into a concise and well-written resume so that your qualifications and potential as an employee will be understood easily and quickly by a complete stranger.

Writing the resume is just one step in what can be a daunting job-search process, but it is an important element in the chain of events that will lead you to your new position. While you are probably a talented, bright, and charming person, your resume may not reflect these qualities. A poorly written resume can get you nowhere; a well-written resume can land you an interview and potentially a job. A good resume can even lead the interviewer to ask you questions that will allow you to talk about your strengths and highlight the skills you can bring to a prospective employer. Even a person with very little experience can find a good job if he or she is assisted by a thoughtful and polished resume.

Lengthy, typewritten resumes are a thing of the past. Today, employers do not have the time or the patience for verbose documents; they look for tightly composed, straightforward, action-based resumes. Although a one-page resume is the norm, a two-page resume may be warranted if you have had extensive job experience or have changed careers and truly need the space to properly position yourself. If, after careful editing, you still need more than one page to present yourself, it's acceptable to use a second page. A crowded resume that's hard to read would be the worst of your choices.

Distilling your work experience, education, and interests into such a small space requires preparation and thought. This book takes you step-by-step through the process of crafting an effective resume that will stand out in today's competitive marketplace. It serves as a workbook and a place to write down your experiences, while also including the techniques you'll need to pull all the necessary elements together. In the following pages, you'll find many examples of resumes that are specific to your area of interest. Study them for inspiration and find what appeals to you. There are a variety of ways to organize and present your information; inside, you'll find several that will be suitable to your needs. Good luck landing the job of your dreams!

Chapter 1

The Elements of an Effective Resume

An effective resume is composed of information that employers are most interested in knowing about a prospective job applicant. This information is conveyed by a few essential elements. The following is a list of elements that are found in most resumes—some essential, some optional. Later in this chapter, we will further examine the role of each of these elements in the makeup of your resume.

- Heading

- Objective and/or Keyword Section

- Work Experience

- Education

- Honors

- Activities

- Certificates and Licenses

- Publications

- Professional Memberships

- Special Skills

- Personal Information

- References

The first step in preparing your resume is to gather information about yourself and your past accomplishments. Later you will refine this information, rewrite it using effective language, and organize it into an attractive layout. But first, let's take a look at each of these important elements individually so you can judge their appropriateness for your resume.

Heading

Although the heading may seem to be the simplest section of your resume, be careful not to take it lightly. It is the first section your prospective employer will see, and it contains the information she or he will need to contact you. At the very least, the heading must contain your name, your home address, and, of course, a phone number where you can be reached easily.

In today's high-tech world, many of us have multiple ways that we can be contacted. You may list your e-mail address if you are reasonably sure the employer makes use of this form of communication. Keep in mind, however, that others may have access to your e-mail messages if you send them from an account provided by your current company. If this is a concern, do not list your work e-mail address on your resume. If you are able to take calls at your current place of business, you should include your work number, because most employers will attempt to contact you during typical business hours.

If you have voice mail or a reliable answering machine at home or at work, list its number in the heading and make sure your greeting is professional and clear. Always include at least one phone number in your heading, even if it is a temporary number, where a prospective employer can leave a message.

You might have a dozen different ways to be contacted, but you do not need to list all of them. Confine your numbers or addresses to those that are the easiest for the prospective employer to use and the simplest for you to retrieve.

Objective

When seeking a specific career path, it is important to list a job or career objective on your resume. This statement helps employers know the direction you see yourself taking, so they can determine whether your goals are in line with those of their organization and the position available. Normally, an objective is one to two sentences long. Its contents will vary depending on your career field, goals, and personality. The objective can be specific or general, but it should always be to the point. See the sample resumes in this book for examples.

If you are planning to use this resume online, or you suspect your potential employer is likely to scan your resume, you will want to include a "keyword" in the objective. This allows a prospective employer, searching hundreds of resumes for a specific skill or position objective, to locate the keyword and find your resume. In essence, a keyword is what's "hot" in your particular field at a given time. It's a buzzword, a shorthand way of getting a particular message across at a glance. For example, if you are a lawyer, your objective might state your desire to work in the area of corporate litigation. In this case, someone searching for the keyword "corporate litigation" will pull up your resume and know that you want to plan, research, and present cases at trial on behalf of the corporation. If your objective states that you "desire a challenging position in systems design," the keyword is "systems design," an industry-specific shorthand way of saying that you want to be involved in assessing the need for, acquiring, and implementing high-technology systems. These are keywords and every industry has them, so it's becoming more and more important to include a few in your resume. (You may need to conduct additional research to make sure you know what keywords are most likely to be used in your desired industry, profession, or situation.)

There are many resume and job-search sites online. Like most things in the online world, they vary a great deal in quality. Use your discretion. If you plan to apply for jobs online or advertise your availability this way, you will want to design a scannable resume. This type of resume uses a format that can be easily scanned into a computer and added to a database. Scanning allows a prospective employer to use keywords to quickly review each applicant's experience and skills, and (in the event that there are many candidates for the job) to keep your resume for future reference.

Many people find that it is worthwhile to create two or more versions of their basic resume. You may want an intricately designed resume on high-quality paper to mail or hand out *and* a resume that is designed to be scanned into a computer and saved on a database or an online job site. You can even create a resume in ASCII text to e-mail to prospective employers. For further information, you may wish to refer to the *Guide to Internet Job Searching*, by Margaret Riley Dikel and Frances E. Roehm, updated and published every other year by VGM Career Books, a division of the McGraw-Hill Companies. This excellent book contains helpful and detailed information about formatting a resume for Internet use. To get you started, in Chapter 3 we have included a list of things to keep in mind when creating electronic resumes.

Although it is usually a good idea to include an objective, in some cases this element is not necessary. The goal of the objective statement is to provide the employer with an idea of where you see yourself going in the field. However, if you are uncertain of the exact nature of the job you seek, including an objective that is too specific could result in your not being considered for a host of perfectly acceptable positions. If you decide not to use an objective heading in your resume, you should definitely incorporate the information that would be conveyed in the objective into your cover letter.

Work Experience

Work experience is arguably the most important element of them all. Unless you have accumulated little or no relevant work experience, your current and former positions will provide the central focus of the resume. You will want this section to be as complete and carefully constructed as possible. By thoroughly examining your work experience, you can get to the heart of your accomplishments and present them in a way that demonstrates and highlights your qualifications.

As you are just entering the workforce, your resume will probably focus on your education, but you should also include information on your work or volunteer experiences. Although you will have less information about work experience than a person who has held multiple positions or is advanced in his or her career, the amount of information is not what is most important in this section. How the information is presented and what it says about you as a worker and a person are what really count.

As you create this section of your resume, remember the need for accuracy. Include all the necessary information about each of your jobs, including your job title, dates of employment, name of your employer, city, state, responsibilities, special projects you handled, and accomplishments. Be sure to list only accomplishments for which you were directly responsible. And don't be alarmed if you haven't participated in or worked on special projects, because this section may not be relevant to certain jobs.

The most common way to list your work experience is in *reverse chronological order*. In other words, start with your most recent job and work your way backward. This way, your prospective employer sees your current (and often most important) position before considering your past employment. Your most recent position, if it's the most important in terms of responsibilities and relevance to the job for which you are applying, should also be the one that includes the most information as compared to your previous positions.

Even if the work itself seems unrelated to your proposed career path, you should list any job or experience that will help sell your talents. If you were promoted or given greater responsibilities or commendations, be sure to mention the fact.

The following worksheet is provided to help you organize your experiences in the working world. It will also serve as an excellent resource to refer to when preparing your resume in the future.

WORK EXPERIENCE

Job One:

Job Title _____

Dates _____

Employer _____

City, State _____

Major Duties _____

_____

_____

_____

_____

_____

_____

_____

_____

Special Projects _____

_____

_____

_____

Accomplishments _____

_____

_____

_____

_____

_____

Job Two:

Job Title _____

Dates _____

Employer _____

City, State _____

Major Duties _____

_____

_____

_____

_____

_____

_____

Special Projects _____

_____

_____

_____

Accomplishments _____

_____

_____

_____

_____

_____

_____

_____

Job Three:

Job Title _____

Dates _____

Employer _____

City, State _____

Major Duties _____

_____

_____

_____

_____

_____

_____

_____

Special Projects _____

_____

_____

_____

Accomplishments _____

_____

_____

_____

_____

_____

_____

_____

Job Four:

Job Title _____

Dates _____

Employer _____

City, State _____

Major Duties _____

_____

_____

_____

_____

_____

_____

_____

Special Projects _____

_____

_____

_____

Accomplishments _____

_____

_____

_____

_____

_____

_____

_____

Education

Education is usually the second most important element of a resume. Your educational background is often a deciding factor in an employer's decision to interview you. Highlight your accomplishments in school as much as you did those accomplishments at work. As you are looking for your first professional job, your education or life experience will be your greatest asset because your related work experience will be minimal. In this case, the education section becomes the most important means of selling yourself.

Include in this section all the degrees or certificates you have received; your major or area of concentration; all of the honors you earned; and any relevant activities you participated in, organized, or chaired. Again, list your most recent schooling first. If you have completed graduate-level work, begin with that and work your way back through your undergraduate education. If you have completed college, you generally should not list your high school experience; do so only if you earned special honors, you had a grade point average that was much better than the norm, or this was your highest level of education.

If you have completed a large number of credit hours in a subject that may be relevant to the position you are seeking but did not obtain a degree, you may wish to list the hours or classes you completed. Keep in mind, however, that you may be asked to explain why you did not finish the program. If you are currently in school, list the degree, certificate, or license you expect to obtain and the projected date of completion.

The following worksheet will help you gather the information you need for this section of your resume.

EDUCATION

School One _____

Major or Area of Concentration _____

Degree _____

Dates _____

School Two _____

Major or Area of Concentration _____

Degree _____

Dates _____

Honors

If you include an honors section in your resume, you should highlight any awards, honors, or memberships in honorary societies that you have received. (You may also incorporate this information into your education section.) Often, the honors are academic in nature, but this section also may be used for special achievements in sports, clubs, or other school activities. Always include the name of the organization awarding the honor and the date(s) received. Use the following worksheet to help you gather your information.

HONORS

Honor One _____

Awarding Organization _____

Date(s) _____

Honor Two _____

Awarding Organization _____

Date(s) _____

Honor Three _____

Awarding Organization _____

Date(s) _____

Honor Four _____

Awarding Organization _____

Date(s) _____

Honor Five _____

Awarding Organization _____

Date(s) _____

Activities

Perhaps you have been active in different organizations or clubs; often an employer will look at such involvement as evidence of initiative, dedication, and good social skills. Examples of your ability to take a leading role in a group should be included on a resume, if you can provide them. The activities section of your resume should present neighborhood and community activities, volunteer positions, and so forth. In general, you may want to avoid listing any organization whose name indicates the race, creed, sex, age, marital status, sexual orientation, or nation of origin of its members because this could expose you to discrimination. Use the following worksheet to list the specifics of your activities.

ACTIVITIES

Organization/Activity _____

Accomplishments _____

_____

_____

Organization/Activity _____

Accomplishments _____

_____

_____

Organization/Activity _____

Accomplishments _____

_____

_____

As your work experience grows through the years, your school activities and honors will carry less weight and be emphasized less in your resume. Eventually, you will probably list only your degree and any major honors received. As time goes by, your job performance and the experience you've gained become the most important elements in your resume, which should change to reflect this.

Certificates and Licenses

If your chosen career path requires specialized training, you may already have certificates or licenses. You should list these if the job you are seeking requires them and you, of course, have acquired them. If you have applied for a license but have not yet received it, use the phrase "application pending."

License requirements vary by state. If you have moved or are planning to relocate to another state, check with that state's board or licensing agency for all licensing requirements.

Always make sure that all of the information you list is completely accurate. Locate copies of your certificates and licenses, and check the exact date and name of the accrediting agency. Use the following worksheet to organize the necessary information.

CERTIFICATES AND LICENSES

Name of License _____

Licensing Agency _____

Date Issued _____

Name of License _____

Licensing Agency _____

Date Issued _____

Name of License _____

Licensing Agency _____

Date Issued _____

Publications

Some professions strongly encourage or even require that you publish. If you have written, coauthored, or edited any books, articles, professional papers, or works of a similar nature that pertain to your field, you will definitely want to include this element. Remember to list the date of publication and the publisher's name, and specify whether you were the sole author or a coauthor. Book, magazine, or journal titles are generally italicized, while the titles of articles within a larger publication appear in quotes. (Check with your reference librarian for more about the appropriate way to present this information.) For scientific or research papers, you will need to give the date, place, and audience to whom the paper was presented.

Use the following worksheet to help you gather the necessary information about your publications.

PUBLICATIONS

Title and Type (Note, Article, etc.) _____

Title of Publication (Journal, Book, etc.) _____

Publisher _____

Date Published _____

Title and Type (Note, Article, etc.) _____

Title of Publication (Journal, Book, etc.) _____

Publisher _____

Date Published _____

Title and Type (Note, Article, etc.) _____

Title of Publication (Journal, Book, etc.) _____

Publisher _____

Date Published _____

Professional Memberships

Another potential element in your resume is a section listing professional memberships. Use this section to describe your involvement in professional associations, unions, and similar organizations. It is to your advantage to list any professional memberships that pertain to the job you are seeking. Many employers see your membership as representative of your desire to stay up-to-date and connected in your field. Include the dates of your involvement and whether you took part in any special activities or held any offices within the organization. Use the following worksheet to organize your information.

PROFESSIONAL MEMBERSHIPS

Name of Organization _____

Office(s) Held_____

Activities _____

Dates _____

Name of Organization _____

Office(s) Held_____

Activities _____

Dates _____

Name of Organization _____

Office(s) Held_____

Activities _____

Dates _____

Name of Organization _____

Office(s) Held_____

Activities _____

Dates _____

Special Skills

The special skills section of your resume is the place to mention any special abilities you have that relate to the job you are seeking. You can use this element to present certain talents or experiences that are not necessarily a part of your education or work experience. Common examples include fluency in a foreign language, extensive travel abroad, or knowledge of a particular computer application. "Special skills" can encompass a wide range of talents, and this section can be used creatively. However, for each skill you list, you should be able to describe how it would be a direct asset in the type of work you're seeking because employers may ask just that in an interview. If you can't think of a way to do this, it may be extraneous information.

Personal Information

Some people include personal information on their resumes. This is generally not recommended, but you might wish to include it if you think that something in your personal life, such as a hobby or talent, has some bearing on the position you are seeking. This type of information is often referred to at the beginning of an interview, when it may be used as an icebreaker. Of course, personal information regarding your age, marital status, race, religion, or sexual orientation should never appear on your resume as personal information. It should be given only in the context of memberships and activities, and only when doing so would not expose you to discrimination.

References

References are not usually given on the resume itself, but a prospective employer needs to know that you have references who may be contacted if necessary. All you need to include is a single sentence at the end of the resume: "References are available upon request," or even simply, "References available." Have a reference list ready—your interviewer may ask to see it! Contact each person on the list ahead of time to see whether it is all right for you to use him or her as a reference. This way, the person has a chance to think about what to say *before* the call occurs. This helps ensure that you will obtain the best reference possible.

Chapter 2

Writing Your Resume

Now that you have gathered the information for each section of your resume, it's time to write it out in a way that will get the attention of the reviewer—hopefully, your future employer! The language you use in your resume will affect its success, so you must be careful and conscientious. Translate the facts you have gathered into the active, precise language of resume writing. You will be aiming for a resume that keeps the reader's interest and highlights your accomplishments in a concise and effective way.

Resume writing is unlike any other form of writing. Although your seventh-grade composition teacher would not approve, the rules of punctuation and sentence building are often completely ignored. Instead, you should try for a functional, direct writing style that focuses on the use of verbs and other words that imply action on your part. Writing with action words and strong verbs characterizes you to potential employers as an energetic, active person, someone who completes tasks and achieves results from his or her work. Resumes that do not make use of action words can sound passive and stale. These resumes are not effective and do not get the attention of any employer, no matter how qualified the applicant. Choose words that display your strengths and demonstrate your initiative. The following list of commonly used verbs will help you create a strong resume:

administered	assembled
advised	assumed responsibility
analyzed	billed
arranged	built

carried out   inspected

channeled   interviewed

collected   introduced

communicated   invented

compiled   maintained

completed   managed

conducted   met with

contacted   motivated

contracted   negotiated

coordinated   operated

counseled   orchestrated

created   ordered

cut   organized

designed   oversaw

determined   performed

developed   planned

directed   prepared

dispatched   presented

distributed   produced

documented   programmed

edited   published

established   purchased

expanded   recommended

functioned as   recorded

gathered   reduced

handled   referred

hired   represented

implemented   researched

improved   reviewed

saved	supervised
screened	taught
served as	tested
served on	trained
sold	typed
suggested	wrote

Let's look at two examples that differ only in their writing style. The first resume section is ineffective because it does not use action words to accent the applicant's work experiences.

WORK EXPERIENCE
Regional Sales Manager

Manager of sales representatives from seven states. Manager of twelve food chain accounts in the East. In charge of the sales force's planned selling toward specific goals. Supervisor and trainer of new sales representatives. Consulting for customers in the areas of inventory management and quality control.

Special Projects: Coordinator and sponsor of annual food-industry sales seminar.

Accomplishments: Monthly regional volume went up 25 percent during my tenure while, at the same time, a proper sales/cost ratio was maintained. Customer–company relations were improved.

In the following paragraph, we have rewritten the same section using action words. Notice how the tone has changed. It now sounds stronger and more active. This person accomplished goals and really *did* things.

WORK EXPERIENCE
Regional Sales Manager

Managed sales representatives from seven states. Oversaw twelve food chain accounts in the eastern United States. Directed the sales force in planned selling toward specific goals. Supervised and trained new sales representatives. Counseled customers in the areas of inventory management and quality control. Coordinated and sponsored the annual Food Industry Seminar. Increased monthly regional volume by 25 percent and helped to improve customer-company relations during my tenure.

One helpful way to construct the work experience section is to make use of your actual job descriptions—the written duties and expectations your employers had for a person in your current or former position. Job descriptions are rarely written in proper resume language, so you will have to rework them, but they do include much of the information necessary to create this section of your resume. If you have access to job descriptions for your former positions, you can use the details to construct an action-oriented paragraph. Often, your human resources department can provide a job description for your current position.

The following is an example of a typical human resources job description, followed by a rewritten version of the same description employing action words and specific details about the job. Again, pay attention to the style of writing instead of the content, as the details of your own experience will be unique.

WORK EXPERIENCE
Public Administrator I

Responsibilities: Coordinate and direct public services to meet the needs of the nation, state, or community. Analyze problems; work with special committees and public agencies; recommend solutions to governing bodies.

Aptitudes and Skills: Ability to relate to and communicate with people; solve complex problems through analysis; plan, organize, and implement policies and programs. Knowledge of political systems, financial management, personnel administration, program evaluation, and organizational theory.

WORK EXPERIENCE
Public Administrator I

Wrote pamphlets and conducted discussion groups to inform citizens of legislative processes and consumer issues. Organized and supervised 25 interviewers. Trained interviewers in effective communication skills.

After you have written out your resume, you are ready to begin the next important step: assembly and layout.

Chapter 3

Assembly and Layout

At this point, you've gathered all the necessary information for your resume and rewritten it in language that will impress your potential employers. Your next step is to assemble the sections in a logical order and lay them out on the page neatly and attractively to achieve the desired effect: getting the interview.

Assembly

The order of the elements in a resume makes a difference in its overall effect. Clearly, you would not want to bury your name and address somewhere in the middle of the resume. Nor would you want to lead with a less important section, such as special skills. Put the elements in an order that stresses your most important accomplishments and the things that will be most appealing to your potential employer. For example, you are new to the workforce, so you will want the reviewer to read about your education and life skills before any part-time jobs you may have held for short durations. On the other hand, once you have been gainfully employed for several years and hold an important position in your company, you should list your work accomplishments ahead of your educational information, which has become less pertinent with time.

Certain things should always be included in your resume, but others are optional. The following list shows you which are which. You might want to use it as a checklist to be certain that you have included all of the necessary information.

Essential	**Optional**
Name	Cellular Phone Number
Address	Pager Number
Phone Number	E-Mail Address or Website Address
Work Experience	Voice Mail Number
Education	Job Objective
References Phrase	Honors
	Special Skills
	Publications
	Professional Memberships
	Activities
	Certificates and Licenses
	Personal Information
	Graphics
	Photograph

Your choice of optional sections depends on your own background and employment needs. Always use information that will put you in a favorable light—unless it's absolutely essential, avoid anything that will prompt the interviewer to ask questions about your weaknesses or something else that could be unflattering. Make sure your information is accurate and truthful. If your honors are impressive, include them in the resume. If your activities in school demonstrate talents that are necessary for the job you are seeking, allow space for a section on activities. If you are applying for a position that requires ornamental illustration, you may want to include border illustrations or graphics that demonstrate your talents in this area. If you are answering an advertisement for a job that requires certain physical traits, a photo of yourself might be appropriate. A person applying for a job as a computer programmer would *not* include a photo as part of his or her resume. Each resume is unique, just as each person is unique.

Types of Resumes

So far we have focused on the most common type of resume—the *reverse chronological* resume—in which your most recent job is listed first. This is the type of resume usually preferred by those who have to read a large number of resumes, and it is by far the most popular and widely circulated. However, this style of presentation may not be the most effective way to highlight *your* skills and accomplishments.

For example, if you are reentering the workforce after many years or are trying to change career fields, the *functional* resume may work best. This type of resume puts the focus on your achievements instead of the sequence of your work history. In the functional resume, your experience is presented through your general accomplishments and the skills you have developed in your working life.

A functional resume is assembled from the same information you gathered in Chapter 1. The main difference lies in how you organize the information. Essentially, the work experience section is divided in two, with your job duties and accomplishments constituting one section and your employers' names, cities, and states; your positions; and the dates employed making up the other. Place the first section near the top of your resume, just below your job objective (if used), and call it *Accomplishments* or *Achievements*. The second section, containing the bare essentials of your work history, should come after the accomplishments section and can be called *Employment History*, since it is a chronological overview of your former jobs.

The other sections of your resume remain the same. The work experience section is the only one affected in the functional format. By placing the section that focuses on your achievements at the beginning, you draw attention to these achievements. This puts less emphasis on where you worked and when, and more on what you did and what you are capable of doing.

If you are changing careers, the emphasis on skills and achievements is important. The identities of previous employers (who aren't part of your new career field) need to be downplayed. A functional resume can help accomplish this task. If you are reentering the workforce after a long absence, a functional resume is the obvious choice. And if you lack full-time work experience, you will need to draw attention away from this fact and put the focus on your skills and abilities. You may need to highlight your volunteer activities and part-time work. Education may also play a more important role in your resume.

The type of resume that is right for you will depend on your personal circumstances. It may be helpful to create both types and then compare them. Which one presents you in the best light? Examples of both types of resumes are included in this book. Use the sample resumes in Chapter 5 to help you decide on the content, presentation, and look of your own resume.

Resume or Curriculum Vitae?

A curriculum vitae (CV) is a longer, more detailed synopsis of your professional history, which generally runs three or more pages in length. It includes a summary of your educational and academic background as well as teaching and research experience, publications, presentations, awards, honors, affiliations, and other details. Because the purpose of the CV is different from that of the resume, many of the rules we've discussed thus far involving style and length do not apply.

A curriculum vitae is used primarily for admissions applications to graduate or professional schools, independent consulting in a variety of settings, proposals for fellowships or grants, or applications for positions in academia. As with a resume, you may need different versions of a CV for different types of positions. You should only send a CV when one is specifically requested by an employer or institution.

Like a resume, your CV should include your name, contact information, education, skills, and experience. In addition to the basics, a CV includes research and teaching experience, publications, grants and fellowships, professional associations and licenses, awards, and other information relevant to the position for which you are applying. You can follow the advice presented thus far to gather and organize your personal information.

Special Tips for Electronic Resumes

Because there are many details to consider in writing a resume that will be posted or transmitted on the Internet, or one that will be scanned into a computer when it is received, we suggest that you refer to the *Guide to Internet Job Searching* as previously mentioned. However, here are some brief, general guidelines to follow if you expect your resume to be scanned into a computer.

- Use standard fonts in which none of the letters touch.

- Keep in mind that underlining, italics, and fancy scripts may not scan well.

- Use boldface and capitalization to set off elements. Again, make sure letters don't touch. Leave at least a quarter inch between lines of type.

- Keep information and elements at the left margin. Centering, columns, and even indenting may change when the resume is optically scanned.

- Do not use any lines, boxes, or graphics.

- Place the most important information at the top of the first page. If you use two pages, put "Page 1 of 2" at the bottom of the first page and put your name and "Page 2 of 2" at the top of the second page.

- List each telephone number on its own line in the header.

- Use multiple keywords or synonyms for what you do to make sure your qualifications will be picked up if a prospective employer is searching for them. Use nouns that are keywords for your profession.

- Be descriptive in your titles. For example, don't just use "assistant"; use "legal office assistant."

- Make sure the contrast between print and paper is good. Use a high-quality laser printer and white or very light colored 8½-by-11-inch paper.

- Mail a high-quality laser print or an excellent copy. Do not fold or use staples, as this might interfere with scanning. You may, however, use paper clips.

In addition to creating a resume that works well for scanning, you may want to have a resume that can be e-mailed to reviewers. Because you may not know what word processing application the recipient uses, the best format to use is ASCII text. (ASCII stands for "American Standard Code for Information Exchange.") It allows people with very different software platforms to exchange and understand information. (E-mail operates on this principle.) ASCII is a simple, text-only language, which means you can include only simple text. There can be no use of boldface, italics, or even paragraph indentations.

To create an ASCII resume, just use your normal word processing program; when finished, save it as a "text only" document. You will find this option under the "save" or "save as" command. Here is a list of things to *avoid* when crafting your electronic resume:

- Tabs. Use your space bar. Tabs will not work.

- Any special characters, such as mathematical symbols.

- Word wrap. Use hard returns (the return key) to make line breaks.

- Centering or other formatting. Align everything at the left margin.

- Bold or italic fonts. Everything will be converted to plain text when you save the file as a "text only" document.

Check carefully for any mistakes before you save the document as a text file. Spellcheck and proofread it several times; then ask someone with a keen eye to go over it again for you. Remember: the key is to keep it simple. Any attempt to make this resume pretty or decorative may result in a resume that is confusing and hard to read. After you have saved the document, you can cut and paste it into an e-mail or onto a website.

Layout for a Paper Resume

A great deal of care—and much more formatting—is necessary to achieve an attractive layout for your paper resume. There is no single appropriate layout that applies to every resume, but there are a few basic rules to follow in putting your resume on paper:

- Leave a comfortable margin on the sides, top, and bottom of the page (usually one to one and a half inches).

- Use appropriate spacing between the sections (two to three line spaces are usually adequate).

- Be consistent in the *type* of headings you use for different sections of your resume. For example, if you capitalize the heading EMPLOY-MENT HISTORY, don't use initial capitals and underlining for a section of equal importance, such as Education.

- Do not use more than one font in your resume. Stay consistent by choosing a font that is fairly standard and easy to read, and don't change it for different sections. Beware of the tendency to try to make your resume original by choosing fancy type styles; your resume may end up looking unprofessional instead of creative. Unless you are in a very creative and artistic field, you should almost always stick with tried-and-true type styles like Times New Roman and Palatino, which are often used in business writing. In the area of resume styles, conservative is usually the best way to go.

CHRONOLOGICAL RESUME

CHRISTINA LORCA

**609 Kirwan Avenue • Newton, MA 02125
(508) 555-4382 • C.Lorca@xxx.com**

Education

Bachelor of Fine Arts, Dance, 2004
University of Vermont, Alpine Ridge, VT

Honors/Awards

Academic and Talent Scholarships, 2000–2004
Alpine National Honor Society
Dean's List

Dance Experience

2004	Falmouth Festival of Music and Art, Francine Denk
	Excerpts from *Barcarole*, Jared Lima
	Dances of Pearl, Elizabeth Karrol
	Golden Slumbers, Nana Lin-Hong, Reconstructed by Tani Arroyo
2003	Suite from *Hallowed Eve*, Jared Lima
	Heart of Hearts, Susan Nitz
	Dream in Red, Tani Arroyo
2002	*Lady Sings the Blues*, Rena Hartman
	Gyroscope, George Lu
	Synergetic Moments, George Lu
1995–1999	Lin-Hong Dance Company, Morrisville, VT – Director, Nana Lin-Hong

Teaching Experience

2004–present	New England School of Dance, Brockton, MA – Director, Jane Howard. Ballet, Jazz, and Tap for children ages 6 to 14.
1999–2001	Alpine Ridge Dance Center, Alpine Ridge, VT – Director, Kristi Buell. Contemporary, Creative Movement, and "Baby Steps" for toddlers and children ages 3 to 13.

Page 1 of 2

Choreographic Experience

2003	*A Rose Touched by the Sun*
	Navajo Windsong, Co-choreographed with Rebecca Sherman
2002	*Donovan's Dream*

Forms Studied

Ballet, Pointe, Jazz, Tap, Character, Modern/Contemporary, Improvisation, Pom-Pons, Synchronized Swimming

Teachers

Jared Lima, Tani Arroyo, George Lu, Rena Hartman, Cynthia Beckett, Kristi Buell, Allen Bounty, Elizabeth Karrol, Darin Alton, Nana Lin-Hong

Other Experience

New Hampshire Summer Arts Program, West Newton, NH
American Student Dance Conference, Middlebury, CT
Alpine Ridge Summer Dance Workshops, Alpine Ridge, VT

References

Jared Lima
c/o University of Vermont
Wagner Hall, School of Dance
Alpine Ridge, VT 05708

Rena Hartman
c/o University of Vermont
Wagner Hall, School of Dance
Alpine Ridge, VT 05708
R.Hartman@xxx.com

Nana Lin-Hong
Director, Lin-Hong Dance Company
11 Thompson Street
Morrisville, VT 05657

FUNCTIONAL RESUME

James Rayburn
Baritone
432 E. 55th St.
New York, NY 10011
(212) 555-2465

6´2´´, 220 lbs.
Light brown hair, green eyes

Opera Performance
Schaunard, *La Boheme*	Indiana University Opera
Papageno, *The Magic Flute*	Indiana University Opera
Dancaïre, *Carmen*	Hammond Symphony
Riff, *West Side Story*	New Horizons Theater

Roles Prepared
Figaro, *Le Nozze di Figaro*
Valentin, *Faust*
Harlequin, *Ariadne auf Naxos* (German and English)

Awards
Bel Canto Foundation Competition	Second Place Winner
Metropolitan Opera Competition	Regional Finalist
NATS Competition	First Place Winner

Education
Indiana University, Bachelor of Music, 2003
Tanglewood Festival, Fellowship Recipient, 2004

Major Teachers: Franz Heidleberg, Mariana Petro, James Morrison Eady
Master Classes: Thomas Garrett, Robert Marks, Renata Teppo

"Mr. Rayburn . . . negotiated difficult passages with ease and finesse."
—South Bend Tribune

"James Rayburn has an energetic . . . unique style [that] dazzled the audience!"
—New York Post

- Always try to fit your resume on one page. If you are having trouble with this, you may be trying to say too much. Edit out any repetitive or unnecessary information, and shorten descriptions of earlier jobs where possible. Ask a friend you trust for feedback on what seems unnecessary or unimportant. For example, you may have included too many optional sections. Today, with the prevalence of the personal computer as a tool, there is no excuse for a poorly laid out resume. Experiment with variations until you are pleased with the result.

Remember that a resume is not an autobiography. Too much information will only get in the way. The more compact your resume, the easier it will be to review. If a person who is swamped with resumes looks at yours, catches the main points, and then calls you for an interview to fill in some of the details, your resume has already accomplished its task. A clear and concise resume makes for a happy reader and a good impression.

There are times when, despite extensive editing, the resume simply cannot fit on one page. In this case, the resume should be laid out on two pages in such a way that neither clarity nor appearance is compromised. Each page of a two-page resume should be marked clearly: the first should indicate "Page 1 of 2," and the second should include your name and the page number, for example, "Julia Ramirez—Page 2 of 2." The pages should then be stapled together. You may use a smaller font (in the same font as the body of your resume) for the page numbers. Place them at the bottom of page one and the top of page two. Again, spend the time now to experiment with the layout until you find one that looks good to you.

Always show your final layout to other people and ask them what they like or dislike about it, and what impresses them most when they read your resume. Make sure that their responses are the same as what you want to elicit from your prospective employer. If they aren't the same, you should continue to make changes until the necessary information is emphasized.

Proofreading

After you have finished typing the master copy of your resume and before you have it copied or printed, thoroughly check it for typing and spelling errors. Do not place all your trust in your computer's spellcheck function. Use an old editing trick and read the whole resume backward—start at the end and read it right to left and bottom to top. This can help you see the small errors or inconsistencies that are easy to overlook. Take time to do it right because a single error on a document this important can cause the reader to judge your attention to detail in a harsh light.

Have several people look at the finished resume just in case you've missed an error. Don't try to take a shortcut; not having an unbiased set of eyes examine your resume now could mean embarrassment later. Even experienced editors can easily overlook their own errors. Be thorough and conscientious with your proofreading so your first impression is a perfect one.

We have included the following rules of capitalization and punctuation to assist you in the final stage of creating your resume. Remember that resumes often require use of a shorthand style of writing that may include sentences without periods and other stylistic choices that break the standard rules of grammar. Be consistent in each section and throughout the whole resume with your choices.

RULES OF CAPITALIZATION

- Capitalize proper nouns, such as names of schools, colleges, and universities; names of companies; and brand names of products.

- Capitalize major words in the names and titles of books, tests, and articles that appear in the body of your resume.

- Capitalize words in major section headings of your resume.

- Do not capitalize words just because they seem important.

- When in doubt, consult a style manual such as *Words into Type* (Prentice Hall) or *The Chicago Manual of Style* (The University of Chicago Press). Your local library can help you locate these and other reference books. Many computer programs also have grammar help sections.

RULES OF PUNCTUATION

- Use commas to separate words in a series.

- Use a semicolon to separate series of words that already include commas within the series. (For an example, see the first rule of capitalization.)

- Use a semicolon to separate independent clauses that are not joined by a conjunction.

- Use a period to end a sentence.

- Use a colon to show that examples or details follow that will expand or amplify the preceding phrase.

- Avoid the use of dashes.

- Avoid the use of brackets.

- If you use any punctuation in an unusual way in your resume, be consistent in its use.

- Whenever you are uncertain, consult a style manual.

Putting Your Resume in Print

You will need to buy high-quality paper for your printer before you print your finished resume. Regular office paper is not good enough for resumes; the reviewer will probably think it looks flimsy and cheap. Go to an office supply store or copy shop and select a high-quality bond paper that will make a good first impression. Select colors like white, off-white, or possibly a light gray. In some industries, a pastel may be acceptable, but be sure the color and feel of the paper make a subtle, positive statement about you. Nothing in the choice of paper should be loud or unprofessional.

If your computer printer does not reproduce your resume properly and produces smudged or stuttered type, either ask to borrow a friend's or take your disk (or a clean original) to a printer or copy shop for high-quality copying. If you anticipate needing a large number of copies, taking your resume to a copy shop or a printer is probably the best choice.

Hold a sheet of your unprinted bond paper up to the light. If it has a watermark, you will want to point this out to the person helping you with copies; the printing should be done so that the reader can read the print and see the watermark the right way up. Check each copy for smudges or streaks. This is the time to be a perfectionist—the results of your careful preparation will be well worth it.

Chapter 4

The Cover Letter

Once your resume has been assembled, laid out, and printed to your satisfaction, the next and final step before distribution is to write your cover letter. Though there may be instances where you deliver your resume in person, you will usually send it through the mail or online. Resumes sent through the mail always need an accompanying letter that briefly introduces you and your resume. The purpose of the cover letter is to get a potential employer to read your resume, just as the purpose of the resume is to get that same potential employer to call you for an interview.

Like your resume, your cover letter should be clean, neat, and direct. A cover letter usually includes the following information:

1. Your name and address (unless it already appears on your personal letterhead) and your phone number(s); see item 7.

2. The date.

3. The name and address of the person and company to whom you are sending your resume.

4. The salutation ("Dear Mr." or "Dear Ms." followed by the person's last name, or "To Whom It May Concern" if you are answering a blind ad).

5. An opening paragraph explaining why you are writing (for example, in response to an ad, as a follow-up to a previous meeting, at the suggestion of someone you both know) and indicating that you are interested in whatever job is being offered.

6. One or more paragraphs that tell why you want to work for the company and what qualifications and experiences you can bring to the position. This is a good place to mention some detail about

that particular company that makes you want to work for them; this shows that you have done some research before applying.

7. A final paragraph that closes the letter and invites the reviewer to contact you for an interview. This can be a good place to tell the potential employer which method would be best to use when contacting you. Be sure to give the correct phone number and a good time to reach you, if that is important. You may mention here that your references are available upon request.

8. The closing ("Sincerely" or "Yours truly") followed by your signature in a dark ink, with your name typed under it.

Your cover letter should include all of this information and be no longer than one page in length. The language used should be polite, businesslike, and to the point. Don't attempt to tell your life story in the cover letter; a long and cluttered letter will serve only to annoy the reader. Remember that you need to mention only a few of your accomplishments and skills in the cover letter. The rest of your information is available in your resume. If your cover letter is a success, your resume will be read and all pertinent information reviewed by your prospective employer.

Producing the Cover Letter

Cover letters should always be individualized because they are always written to specific individuals and companies. Never use a form letter for your cover letter or copy it as you would a resume. Each cover letter should be unique, and as personal and lively as possible. (Of course, once you have written and rewritten your first cover letter until you are satisfied with it, you can certainly use similar wording in subsequent letters. You may want to save a template on your computer for future reference.) Keep a hard copy of each cover letter so you know exactly what you wrote in each one.

There are sample cover letters in Chapter 6. Use them as models or for ideas of how to assemble and lay out your own cover letters. Remember that every letter is unique and depends on the particular circumstances of the individual writing it and the job for which he or she is applying.

After you have written your cover letter, proofread it as thoroughly as you did your resume. Again, spelling or punctuation errors are a sure sign of carelessness, and you don't want that to be a part of your first impression on a prospective employer. This is no time to trust your spellcheck function. Even after going through a spelling and grammar check, your cover letter should be carefully proofread by at least one other person.

Print the cover letter on the same quality bond paper you used for your resume. Remember to sign it, using a good dark-ink pen. Handle the letter and resume carefully to avoid smudging or wrinkling, and mail them together in an appropriately sized envelope. Many stores sell matching envelopes to coordinate with your choice of bond paper.

Keep an accurate record of all resumes you send out and the results of each mailing. This record can be kept on your computer, in a calendar or notebook, or on file cards. Knowing when a resume is likely to have been received will keep you on track as you make follow-up phone calls.

About a week after mailing resumes and cover letters to potential employers, contact them by telephone. Confirm that your resume arrived and ask whether an interview might be possible. Be sure to record the name of the person you spoke to and any other information you gleaned from the conversation. It is wise to treat the person answering the phone with a great deal of respect; sometimes the assistant or receptionist has the ear of the person doing the hiring.

You should make a great impression with the strong, straightforward resume and personalized cover letter you have just created. We wish you every success in securing the career of your dreams!

Sample Resumes

This chapter contains dozens of sample resumes for people pursuing a wide variety of jobs and careers.

There are many different styles of resumes in terms of graphic layout and presentation of information. These samples represent people with varying amounts of education and experience. Use them as models for your own resume. Choose one resume or borrow elements from several different resumes to help you design your own.

Denise T. Bodeane
1221 East Cambridge Avenue
Lynn, MA 01901
dbodeane@xxx.com
617-555-8800

Objective
To obtain a position as a publicist with an arts organization.

Work History
Boston Opera Company, Boston, MA
Publicist, January 2004–Present
- Compose press releases and public service announcements that publicize opera events.
- Develop contacts with Boston entertainment columnists that result in extensive coverage.
- Maintain calendar of advertising deadlines.
- Write copy for print and radio advertisements.

Sandra Watt Agency, Boston, MA
Editorial/P.R. Assistant, November 2001–December 2003
- Edited technical and literary manuscripts.
- Compiled a directory of Boston editors and publishers for agency use.
- Organized an educational workshop for local writers.

Education
- Ithaca University, Ithaca, New York
- B.S. in Advertising, June 2001
- Courses: Marketing Techniques, Advertising, Corporate Public Relations, P.R. Techniques

Honors
- Sigma Kappa Nu Honorary Society
- Honors in Advertising
- Dean's List
- Myron T. Kapp Public Relations Award

Activities
- Student Government Representative
- Homecoming Committee
- Soccer Club

References provided on request.

ALLISON SPRINGS

15 Hilton House • Colorado Women's College
Denver, CO 80220
Home: 303-555-2550 • Cellular: 303-555-8890

JOB SOUGHT

To obtain a position within a government or nonprofit agency that can benefit from my organizational and marketing skills.

SKILLS AND EXPERIENCE

NEGOTIATING SKILLS

Developed negotiating skills through participation in student government. Acted as leader and moderator of various committees.

PROMOTIONAL SKILLS

Contributed greatly to my successful campaign for class office (Junior Class Vice President) through the effective use of posters, displays, and other visual aids. Participated in committee projects as well as fund-raising efforts that netted $15,000 for the junior class project.

PEOPLE SKILLS

As Junior Class Vice President, I balanced the concerns of different groups in order to reach a common goal. As a claims interviewer with a state public assistance agency, I dealt with people under stressful circumstances. While a research assistant with a law firm, I interacted with both lawyers and clerical workers and managed the needs of both. As a lifeguard, I learned how to manage groups and lead activities.

EDUCATION

Colorado Women's College
Bachelor of Arts in Political Science
Degree expected June 2005
Junior Class Vice President
Student Council
Harvest Committee

WORK EXPERIENCE

McCall, Davis & Jones, Westrow, CO
Research Assistant, January 2003-present

Department of Public Assistance, Denver, CO
Claims Interviewer, September 2003-December 2003

Shilo Pool, Shilo, NE
Lifeguard, Summers 2000-2003

Stan Beltzman

572 First Street • Brooklyn, NY 11215 • s.beltzman@xxx.com • 718-555-4328

Education:

Princeton University, Princeton, NJ
Degree Expected: M.S. in Communications, June 2005
Class Rank: Top 10 percent
Editor of *Communications Journal*

University of Wisconsin, Madison, WI
B.A. in Political Science, May 2003
Dean's List
Marching Band Section Leader

Work History:

Boston Theatre Co., Boston, MA
P.R. Internship, June 2004 to September 2004
*Composed press releases and public service
announcements publicizing theatre events. Oversaw
production of posters, flyers, and programs. Sold sub-
scriptions and advertising space.*

Other Experience:

Citizens Action Group, New York, NY
Field Manager, June 2003 to September 2003
*Promoted public awareness of state legislative process
and issues of toxic waste, utility control, and consumer
legislation. Demonstrated effective fund-raising skills.*

University of Wisconsin, Madison, WI
Resident Assistant, Office of Residential Life
September 2002 to June 2003
*Administered all aspects of student affairs and univer-
sity residence halls, including program planning, disci-
pline, and individual group counseling. Directed
achievement of student goals through guidance of
the residence hall council. Implemented all university
policies.*

University of Wisconsin, Madison, WI
Staff Training Lecturer, August 2002 to December 2002
*Conducted workshops for residence hall staff on coun-
seling, effective communication, and conflict resolution.*

Special Skills:

• Knowledge of Microsoft Office, including Word, Excel,
  and PowerPoint
• Knowledge of Spanish and French
• CPR certified

Terrence Wallace

700 Thornborough Road
Chattanooga, TN 37415
Terry.Wallace@xxx.com
615-555-2111

Career Objective

To obtain a career in the field of broadcast journalism in which I can utilize my experience in writing, editing, and research.

Education

Howard University, Washington, DC
Bachelor of Arts, Journalism
June 2004

Work Experience

WDC-TV, Washington, DC
Research Assistant, News Department, Summer 2003
Assisted in all aspects of the production of a news show.
Served as a copy aide.
Worked at UPI office during congressional hearings.
Handled general research duties.

Capitol Magazine, Washington, DC
Editorial Assistant to Senior Editor, Summer 2002
Coordinated an organized system of manuscript flow between editors.
Assisted in editing and proofreading copy.
Rewrote news articles and planned new stories and layout ideas.

Chattanooga News, Chattanooga, TN
Intern, Summer 2001
Assisted in layout, editing, and reporting for local newspaper.
Wrote and edited articles.

Park Advertising, Inc., Chattanooga, TN
Creative Department Intern, Summer 2000
Handled proofreading and editing of copy.
Assisted in various types of demographic research.

Honors

Harris Academic Scholarship: 2002, 2003
Dean's List

References

Available on request.

Eduardo Lopez

6 East Columbus Drive • College Park, MD 20740

E.Lopez@xxx.com • 410-555-3938

Goal

To obtain a research technician position that allows me to use my training in physics.

Education

University of Maryland, College Park, MD
Bachelor of Science—Physics, June 2004

Relevant Course Work

Plasma Physics
Medical Instrumentation
Advanced Statistics
Research Methodology

Honors

Dean's List
Sigma Pi Sigma, Physics Honor Society

Experience

University of Maryland, Physics Department—Research Associate
June 2004 to Present
- Conduct literature research and create literature studies to support work of department.
- Record and analyze research data.
- Contribute to technical reports and publications.

Huntington Burroughs Pharmaceutical Inc.—Student Intern
Summer 2003
- Assisted the senior researcher with all aspects of data input, statistical analysis, and computer model development.

References

Available on request.

Angelo Cruciano

3233 North Lincoln Avenue • Chicago, IL 60657

Home: 773-555-2029 • E-mail: a.cruciano@xxx.com

Goal
To obtain a position in marketing and publicity within the recording industry.

Work History
PTO Productions, Evanston, IL
Public Relations/Marketing Assistant
May 2004 to Present
- Assist P.R. Director with all duties, including radio promotion and retail marketing.
- Coordinate radio and print interviews for artists.
- Manage all details of office including scheduling, record keeping, and document preparation.

WCHO Radio, Chicago, IL
Music Director
June 2003 to May 2004
- Selected appropriate music for a contemporary jazz format.
- Oversaw daily operations of music library and programming department.
- Supervised a staff of six.

Education
Northwestern University, Evanston, IL
B.A. in Arts Management, May 2004
- Ross Hunter Arts Management Scholarship
- GPA in major: 3.8

Skills
- Fluent in French
- Knowledge of Microsoft Word, Excel, and PowerPoint
- Experience in database management

References
On request

Andrew Roberts

998 Essex Boulevard, Apt. 32 • Toledo, OH 43601
Andy.Roberts@xxx.com • 419-555-4098

Objective
To obtain a position in the field of finance.

Education
Western University, Toledo, OH
Graduate School of Business Administration
M.B.A. expected in June 2004
• Concentration: Finance
• Finance Club
• Student Advisory Board

University of Illinois at Chicago, Chicago, IL
B.A. in Economics, June 2002
• Summa Cum Laude
• Phi Beta Kappa
• Student Government Vice President

Work Experience
First Family Bank, Chicago, IL
Financial Associate, September 2003 to Present
• Review and process loan applications, including establishing collateral,
  checking credit ratings, and verifying employment status.
• Discuss loan terms with new customers and handle all related paperwork.

Bank of Ohio, Toledo, OH
Commercial Loan Intern, Summer 2002
• Provided financial data to commercial account officers.
• Handled past-due receivables.

University of Illinois, Chicago, IL
Assistant, Accounts Payable Department, 2001 to 2002
• Assisted with data input, check requests, and disbursements.
• Tracked accounts receivable and accounts payable.

References available upon request.

Belinda S. Browne

66 Overland Avenue • Toledo, OH 43601
B.Browne@xxx.com • 419-555-3600

Career Goal
To obtain a position as an assistant auditor

Education
University of Toledo, Toledo, OH
Master of Science in Accounting
Expected December 2005

Experience
Marino and Associates, Toledo, OH
Internship, January 2004-May 2004
Prepared audit risk analyses
Handled routine account reviews
Organized client records

Membership
American Institute of Certified Public Accountants (Student)

References
Submitted upon request

Travis Shavers

15 E. Greenview St., Apt. 333
Richmond, VA 23229
T.Shavers@xxx.com
804-555-3903

Education
University of Virginia, Richmond, VA
B.A. in Journalism, expected June 2005

Hawkins Journalism Scholarship, 2003 and 2004
Intern with WRCH-TV
Vice President, Senior Class

Writing Experience
- Served as senior editor of campus newspaper--selected articles, approved editorials, edited and wrote copy, supervised seven writers.
- Assisted in the editing of literary magazine *Flight*--proofread and edited copy.
- Wrote a weekly column for campus newspaper--actively pursued investigative reporting, handled events both on campus and in the local community.
- Created design and layout for the 2001 Freshman Handbook--assisted with typesetting and offset printing of handbook.

Work History
University of Virginia, Richmond, VA

Senior Editor, Campus Newspaper, 2004 to Present

Editor, *Flight*, 2004

Writer, Campus Newspaper, 2003 to 2004

Designer, Freshman Handbook, 2001

Memberships
Association of College Journalists
Virginia Literary Society

References available upon request

• Margaret Weidlin •

333 Market Street, Apt. 608
San Francisco, CA 94123
Maggie.Weidlin@xxx.com
415-555-3526

• Job Sought •

Designer of cutting-edge women's fashion

• Education •

Parkwood College of Design, San Francisco, CA
M.A. in Fashion Design, June 2004

Northwestern University, Evanston, IL
B.A. in Art History, 1999

• Employer •

Davie Wear, Inc., San Francisco, CA
Assistant Fashion Coordinator, 2002-Present

• Skills and Accomplishments •

- Prepare clothing for display
- Evaluate and select fabrics
- Design patterns for fabric
- Coordinate window displays

• References •

Susan DeGeorge, Owner
Davie Wear, Inc.
s.degeorge@xxx.com
415-555-5958, ext. 332

Alex Rosenthal, Instructor
Parkwood College of Design
rosenthal@xxx.com
415-555-4900, ext. 839

Design portfolio available upon request.

THEODORE L. MCDONALD

2107 Adams Street, Apt. 9
Austin, TX 78711
t.mcdonald@xxx.com
(512) 555-7665

JOB SOUGHT

Dietitian/Nutritionist

EDUCATION

University of Texas, Austin, TX
B.S. in Nutrition, June 2003

HONORS

Spielberg Nutrition Award
Dean's List, four semesters

EMPLOYMENT HISTORY

University of Texas, Austin, TX
Assistant Nutritionist, September 2001 to Present
• Have planned over 250 menus with Head Nutritionist.
• Oversee interviewing and hiring of student workers.

Austin Hospital, Austin, TX
Assistant to Head Dietitian, Summers 2001 and 2002
• Assisted with menus and meal planning.
• Selected and delivered meals to special-diet patients.

REFERENCES

Available upon Request

Sagu Rugat

888 S. Evers St.
Trenton, NJ 08778
Home: 609-555-4903
Work: 609-555-7366
S.Rugat@xxx.com

Goal

Obtain a position as an assistant editor for a major book publisher.

Education

University of Illinois, Champaign, IL
Bachelor of Arts Degree, English
June 2003
GPA in major: 4.0

Skills

- Familiar with *The Chicago Manual of Style*
- Excellent written and oral communication skills
- Ability to handle and prioritize multiple assignments
- Excellent attention to detail
- Strong computer skills, including Publisher, Photoshop, and Quark

Experience

Curtiss Publishing, Trenton, NJ
Editorial Assistant, August 2003–Present
- Assist editorial staff with all aspects of book production.
- Schedule and track progress of projects.
- Proofread manuscripts.
- Type book contracts and correspondence.
- Read submissions.

University of Illinois Press, Champaign, IL
Student Intern, Summer 2002
- Provided general clerical support for university press.
- Performed fact-checking and proofreading.

References

Available

Stanley Trumbull

3 S. Sioux Tr. • Ottawa, ONT K1P 5N2
stan.trumbull@xxx.com • 613-555-1782

Objective

To obtain a career in the field of anthropology.

Education

University of Ottawa, Ottawa, ONT
B.A. in Anthropology, expected June 2005

Honors

Dean's List, 2004
Phillips Anthropology Award, 2004

Employment History

Ottawa University, Ottowa, ONT
Department of Animal Behavior
Research Assistant, September 2003–Present
• Input data for animal behavior studies.
• Maintained lab equipment.
• Monitored animals and recorded data.

Ottawa University, Ottowa, ONT
Admissions Office
Student Assistant, September 2002–April 2003
• Conducted campus tours.
• Processed applications.
• Assisted in student recruitment and general public relations.

Parker & Parker, Detroit, MI
Office Assistant, June 2002–September 2002
• Handled data entry, processing orders, phones.

Activities

Anthropology Club, 2002–Present
Student Government Representative, Fall 2003

References

Available upon request.

CHRISTINE HARDING

3333 North Halen Avenue, Apt. 3B
Toronto, ONT M6P 4C7
E-mail: c.harding@xxx.com
Home: 416-555-2333

EDUCATION

Toronto School of Law, Toronto, ONT
Juris Doctor, Expected June 2005
Area of Concentration: Health-care Litigation

University of California, Irvine, CA
B.S. in Biology, May 2002
Summa Cum Laude

WORK EXPERIENCE

Tannen & Hope, Toronto, ONT
Intern, January 2003–Present
• Draft legal documents
• Assist in the preparation of cases for trial
• Conduct legal research
• File motions with the court

SKILLS

Fluent in Spanish
Knowledge of Sign Language

MEMBERSHIPS

Student Government Association
Progressive Law Coalition
Kappa Phi Honorary Society

REFERENCES

Provided on request

Rebecca Porter Upjohn

100 West Tenth Street • Bloomington, IN 47401
R.Upjohn@xxx.com • 317-555-3893

Objective
A career in digital photography

Education
Indiana State University, Terre Haute, IN
Bachelor of Arts, Visual Communications, June 2003
Emphasis in Digital Photography

Course Work
Studio Lighting
Bank Lighting
Advertising/Product Photography
Photojournalism
Portrait Photography
Digital Photography and Manipulation

Work Experience
Freelance Photographer, June 2003 to Present
Handle advertising, publication, passport, and portrait photography.

Photographer, Media Center, 2002 to 2003
Indiana State University, Terre Haute, IN
Worked directly with designer to fulfill the university's photographic needs.
Used high-speed film to photograph dramatic events in existing light.
Contributed photographs to university publications.
Mastered standard film processing.

Student Assistant, Bloomington Library, 2001 to 2002
Indiana State University, Terre Haute, IN
Assisted students in locating materials within the library and online.
Worked checkout desk.
Shelved and cataloged new materials.

Page 1 of 2

Exhibits
Community Show, 2003
Campus Center, 2003
Bloomington Library, 2002
Parker Gallery, 2002

Memberships
Women in Photography
Designers in Progress
Communications Club
Advertising Club

Computer Experience
Microsoft Photoshop and Publisher
Quark

Portfolio and References Available

Peter Perkins
60 Martin Drive
Milwaukee, WI 53201
414-555-1111
peterperkins@xxx.com

Objective: A career in the printing field

Education: Institute of Technology, Milwaukee, WI
                          Certificate in offset printing technology,
                          May 2004

Relevant Courses: Machine Design
                          Computers and Printing
                          Planning
                          Manufacturing Analysis

Employment History: Wisconsin Printing Co., Milwaukee, WI
                          Intern, Summers 2002 and 2003
                          Learned operation of Goss C700 and N900
                          presses.
                          Reviewed sample copy material.

                          UPS, West Allis, WI
                          Delivery Person, 2000 to 2002
                          Prepared packages for delivery.
                          Organized truck.
                          Delivered packages.

References: Submitted on request

Bridgett Terry

4444 24th Street   Los Angeles, CA 90061
B.Terry@xxx.com   213-555-3411

Objective
A position in personnel administration.

Education
Human Resources Administration
Lorminon College, Dallas, TX
Certificate of Completion, Summer 2004

University of California at Berkeley, Berkeley, CA
Bachelor's Degree in Economics, 1999

Honors
Personnel Management Institute Dean's Award, 2004
Student Government Secretary, 1998
Gamma Kappa Phi Honorary Society, 1998-1999

Work Experience
Woodbine & Co., Los Angeles, CA
Human Resources Assistant, 2000-Present
• Greet current and prospective employees in the main office.
• Research and evaluate applications.
• Maintain employee referrals.
• File performance appraisals.
• Help write job descriptions.
• Record data on vacations, sick time, and leaves of absence.

Computer Experience
• Entire Microsoft Office Suite, including Work, PowerPoint, Access,
  and Excel.
• Numerous customized databases, including ACT, GELCO, and ADMARC.
• Knowledge of a variety of online research resources.

KRISTINE HINCH

5222 38TH STREET
WASHINGTON, DC 20013
K.HINCH@XXX.COM
202-555-2003

OBJECTIVE

A career in Business Management

EDUCATION

Georgetown University, Washington, DC
M.B.A. expected June 2004
Area of Concentration: Financial Management/Accounting Management

Parker College, Parker, IA
B.A. June 2002
Major: Economics
Minor: Political Science

WORK EXPERIENCE

Georgetown University, Washington, DC
Analytical Studies Intern, 2003 - Present
• Collect and organize data for a university finance study
• Conduct library research
• Contribute to draft of final reports

Parker College, Parker, IA
Resident Hall Assistant, 2000 - 2002
• Oversaw all aspects of a college dormitory
• Supervised residents and kitchen and maintenance staff
• Served as a liaison to the Student Affairs Office

Derek Miller

15 Nob Hill Street • San Francisco, CA 94105

E-mail: D.Miller@xxx.com • (415) 555-4389

Job Objective

Graphic Designer

Work Experience

Derek Miller Design, San Francisco, CA
Freelance Designer, 2002 to Present
Design all aspects of brochures, ads, and posters.
Coordinate all design details for fashion shows.

Berkeley College of Design, Berkeley, CA
Graphic Design Intern, 2001
Designed printed materials for university clients.
Projects included alumni directory and admissions brochure.

Fern Labs, Inc., Berkeley, CA
Graphics Assistant, 2000 to 2001
Designed and produced illustrations for brochures.

University of Minnesota, Minneapolis, MN
Photographer, 1998 to 1999
Took photos for university publications.

Education

Berkeley College of Design, Berkeley, CA
B.A. in Graphic Design, May 2003

University of Minnesota, Minneapolis, MN
B.A. in History, May 1999

Awards

Northern California Photography Exhibit: 3rd Place, 2002
Berkeley Student Design Show: Honorable Mention, 2003

References

Available on Request

Lori Wu

489 McCauley   Oakland, CA 94609
Lori.Wu@xxx.com   Home: (415) 555-7020   Pager: (415) 555-0026

Objective
To obtain a social work position utilizing my experience with youth programs, substance abuse recovery, and/or inmate rehabilitation.

Education
M.S.W., 2002
Stanford University, Palo Alto, CA

B.A. in English, 1999
University of Chicago, Chicago, IL

Course Work
Introduction to Psychology
Social Welfare Systems
Theory of Social Work
Abnormal Psychology
Urban Problems
Case Analysis
History of Social Welfare
Business Management
Topics in Sociology

Fieldwork
Counselor, 2003-Present
Covenant House, Oakland, CA

Interviewer, 2002-2003
Oakland Drug Rehab Program, Oakland, CA

Volunteer, 1999-2000
San Francisco Youth Center, San Francisco, CA

References
Available upon request.

Megan O'Connell

303 13th Street • San Francisco, CA 94114 • moconnell@xxx.com • 415-555-4311

Education
San Francisco State University, San Francisco, CA
B.A. in Communications, expected June 2005
Current GPA of 3.36
Dean's List

Courses
Journalism
Broadcasting
Mass Communications
Public Relations
Film
Child Psychology
Human Behavior
Sociology
English Literature
Child Welfare

Work Experience
Gamma Gamma Phi, San Francisco, CA
Public Relations Assistant, 2003 to Present
• Handle press releases and contacts with chapter members
• Help to establish new branch chapters
• Create and manage database
• Conduct research

Honors
Panda Scholarship
Dean's List
Communications Honor Society
Gamma Gamma Phi

References available on request.

Mohamad Rojad

Permanent Address   **Temporary Address**
South East Hollow Road   150 Ft. Washington Avenue
Berlin, NY 12022   New York, NY 10032
(518) 555-6057   (212) 555-8934

Objective
A management trainee position in the telecommunications industry.

Education
Bachelor of Science, Communications
New York University, New York, NY
Date of Graduation, May 2005
Communications GPA 3.8
Academic GPA 3.5

Professional Experience
Tutor, Self-employed, September 2004 - Present
Help students to better understand the basic concepts of mathematics.

Tax Consultant, V.I.T.A. (Volunteer Income Tax Assistance), Spring 2004
Provided income tax assistance to lower income and elderly taxpayers who were
unable to prepare returns or pay for professional assistance.

Cook, Randy's Seafood, New York, NY, Summer 2003
Prepared and cooked assorted seafood dishes.
Coordinated deliveries and receiving.

Laborer and Driver, Jones Construction, Brooklyn, NY, Summers 2001 and 2002
Operated heavy machinery and handled other aspects including delivering materials
to and from various job sites.

Activities and Honors
Beta Alpha Psi (Communications Honor Society), 2004 - 2005
Dean's List, three semesters
A.I.B. (Association for International Business)
Racquetball and tennis teams

References available upon request.

YOLANDA FINKELSTEIN

5444 S. Magnolia
North Hollywood, CA 91604
818-555-2909
y.finkelstein@xxx.com

OBJECTIVE

A position in interior design and decorative arts

SKILLS

Creative floor plans
Functional design details
Coordinated fabrics and furnishings
Personalized color schemes and textile designs

EMPLOYMENT HISTORY

Magnolia Street Design Studio
Owner
2002-Present

Madigan Textiles
Student Intern
2000-2002

EDUCATION

University of California—Santa Barbara
B.A. in Decorative Arts
Awarded June 2002

REFERENCES

Client list, portfolio, and references are available

➤ *Theonios Petropolus*

8900 Santa Monica Blvd., #802
Los Angeles, CA 90069
Home: 213-555-4098
E-mail: Theo.Petropolus@xxx.com
Website: www.petropolus.com

➤ *Goal*

Programmer/analyst position with opportunity to develop skills in software design.

➤ *Programs*

Cold Fusion, PHP, Apache, Visual Basic/Visual Studio, COM/ActiveX, HTML, JavaScript, XML/XSL, CasheScript, Database Management, ADO, SQL

➤ *Experience*

Colonial Insurance, Programmer, 8/03 to Present
Accomplishments:
Developed mainframe programs to create a download file for pension administration package. Converted and maintained the raw material paper inventory system that tracked $9M paper inventory, from a Honeywell DPS-88 platform on an IBM.

Williams Financial Group, Programmer, 6/02 to 8/03
Accomplishments:
As programmer and project manager for wholesale financial core, developed front-end processor to reformat invoice information into trust finance agreements using multiple IMS databases.

➤ *Education*

Boston College, Bachelor of Science Degree, 6/02
Major: Finance
Minor: Computer and Information Services

➤ *References*

Personal and professional references available.

Mark E. Ruczinski

4330 Chesapeake NW
Washington, DC 20010
Mark.Ruczinski@xxx.com
202-555-1331

Career Goal
Attorney for a mid- to large-sized business law firm.

Education
Pace University
White Plains, NY
J.D., June 2003

Iona College
New Rochelle, NY
M.B.A., June 1998
B.A., June 1994

Professional Qualifications
- Admission to New York Bar, 2003
- Certified Public Accountant, New York, 2000
- Member of the American Institute of CPAs
- Member of the New York Society of CPAs

Business Experience
Greyhound Bus Lines, New York, NY
Assistant General Counsel and Assistant to Treasurer, 2001 to Present
- Handle tax research and planning for the corporation and its subsidiaries.
- Conduct legal research.

City of Washington, Department of Finance
Assistant to Financial Analyst, 2000 to 2001
- Assisted with financial analysis and preparation of financial reports, including the annual financial report and financial schedules for bond prospectuses.

References submitted upon request.

JOHN LEE

3310 15th Street • San Francisco, CA 94114
John.Lee@xxx.com • 415-555-1687

PROFESSIONAL OBJECTIVE

An entry-level position in the field of accounting that will lead to managerial responsibilities

EDUCATION

San Francisco State University, San Francisco, CA
Master of Science, Expected May 2005
Major: Accounting
- Program included independent study of Advanced Accounting Theory, Financial Statement Analysis, and Tax Law
- GPA: 3.5/4.0
- Thesis: Impacts of Economic Recovery

Stanford University, Palo Alto, CA
Bachelor of Science, June 2002
Major: Business

WORK EXPERIENCE

May Co., San Francisco, CA
Department Manager, Men's Clothing, 2002-Present
- Supervise sales staff.
- Hire, train, and monitor new staff.
- Manage shipment and cash management responsibilities.
- Maintain monthly expenses and yearly budgets.
- Create sales analysis reports for use by management and buyers.

References available

harriet schumacher

1414 N. Montebello Dr.   Berkeley, CA 94706
H.Schumacher@xxx.com   (415) 555-4930

education

University of California at Berkeley
Bachelor of Arts in Journalism
Expected: June 2005

honors

Beta Gamma Epsilon Honorary Society
Dean's List
Manley Writing Award, 2004

activities

Treasurer, Gamma Gamma Gamma Sorority
Resident Advisor
Homecoming Planning Committee
Alumni Welcoming Committee

work experience

Berkeley Dispatch
Student Intern, 2003 to Present
Assist in layout, editing, and reporting for local newspaper.
Write and edit articles.
Handle preparatory research for local sports events.

University of California at Berkeley
Office Assistant, Journalism School, 2001 to 2003
Assisted with registration, filing, and typing.
Arranged application materials.
Assembled course packs.

special skills

Fluent in German
Familiar with numerous layout and design programs, including
Photoshop, Publisher, and Quark

Christopher Bernard Smalls

434 N. Wabash Street
Cleveland, Ohio 44102
Chris.Smalls@xxx.com
216-555-6845

Objective
A position as a management trainee in an insurance company

Education
Bachelor of Science in Business Administration
Kent State University, Kent, OH
Expected: June 2005

Honors
Dean's List, four semesters
N. Young Scholarship
Undergraduate Business Award

Work Experience
Allstate Insurance, Cleveland, OH
Receptionist, Summer 2003
Assisted in the areas of research, demographics, signing new customers, and filing claims.

Kent State University, Kent, OH
Research/Office Assistant, 2002-2003
Researched and compiled materials for department professors.
Arranged filing system and supervisor's library.
Organized department inventory.

Special Skills
Fluent in German
Strong communication skills

References available upon request.

Jane Wiggins

1814 N. Seminola Ave., #2442 • Cleveland, OH 44116
J.Wiggins@xxx.com • 216-555-3400

Career Objective

To become a sales representative for an office supplies manufacturer.

Employment History

Tempo Office Supply Co., Cleveland, OH
Executive Secretary to Sales Manager
2002–Present
- Assist the sales manager in various office activities and procedures.
- Handle price quotations, information on product line, customer inquiries on shipments, and special orders.
- Arrange travel, hotel accommodations, and scheduling of seminars and meetings.
- Draft monthly reports on sales procedures and profit margins.
- Manage computerization of the office records.

James Plastics, St. Louis, MO
Secretary to Manager of Publications, 1996–2001
- Arranged conferences for the department.
- Dealt directly with staff members on a variety of matters, including routing editing duties and proof-reading responsibilities.
- Edited and proofread interoffice memos and weekly department newsletter.
- Arranged for printing and distribution.
- Trained and supervised two student interns.

Education

Cleveland University, Cleveland, OH
B.S. in Marketing, 2003 (Evening Division)

St. Louis School of Business, St. Louis, MO
Completed advanced secretarial course, 1996

Special Skills

Proficient in numerous software packages.
Typing speed: 60 wpm.
Knowledge of Spanish.

Carrine Kanka
9370 Trent Drive
Jackson, MS 39208
carrine.kanka@xxx.com
601-555-3898

Job Objective

To obtain a position that will use my writing and editorial skills to promote environmental awareness.

Skills and Accomplishments

- Edited *Save the Planet*, an environmental publication directed at concerned citizens.
- Researched and wrote articles for *Conservation* magazine.
- Wrote technical articles and instructional manuals on software applications, office equipment, and kitchen appliances.
- Edited grant proposals for a local college.

Employment History

Freelance Writer, 2002–Present

Education

Columbia University, Columbia, SC
B.A. in Journalism, June 2003
Minor in History

Special Skills

- Knowledge of Word, Publisher, Photoshop, PowerPoint, and Quark.
- Utilize Windows, Macintosh, and Linux operating systems.
- Working knowledge of French and German.
- Familiar with *AP Stylebook* and *The Chicago Manual of Style*.

References and writing samples available.

Martin C. Chan

64 Collin Road • Miami, FL 33109 • martin.chan@xxx.com • 305-555-7757

Goal

Production Assistant for a film company

Experience

Location scouting
Securing film permits
Locating and managing props
Handling travel arrangements for crews
Supervising extras on location
Assisting producers and location managers
Photographing promotional stills

Employers

New Order Productions, Miami, FL
Production Assistant, 2003–Present

Tert Film Productions, Chicago, IL
Production Coordinator, Summer 2003

Baltimore Film Festival, Baltimore, MD
Production Assistant, Summer 2002

KKSF Radio, Berkeley, CA
Producer, 1999–2003

Education

University of California, Berkeley, CA
B.A. in Film Production, 2003

References

On request

Peter Thomason

Fulton Hall, Room 306
2300 West Harrison
Chicago, IL 60633
pete.thomason@xxx.com
312-555-4849

Objective   *A career in the field of finance*

Education   University of Illinois at Chicago, Chicago, IL
                         Bachelor of Arts in Economics
                         Expected: June 2004

Honors   Phi Beta Kappa
                         Dean's List - five semesters
                         Robeson Business Scholarship, 2003

Activities   Vice President, Beta Gamma Fraternity
                         Teaching Assistant, Accounting Department
                         Baseball Team
                         Student Rights Group

Work Experience   IBM, Northbrook, IL
                         Accounting Intern, 2002
                         Assisted finance department in the areas of computer account-
                         ing, bookkeeping, financial statements, forecasts, and planning.
                         Extensive use of spreadsheet software programs.

                         University of Illinois at Chicago, Chicago, IL
                         Office Assistant, Journalism School, 2001
                         Assisted with registrations, filing, and typing. Arranged applica-
                         tion materials. Prepared course materials for faculty.

Special Skills   Fluent in Japanese
                         Knowledge of statistics
                         Strong computer skills

References   *Available on request*

• Randall Turner •

698 4th Street • Atlanta, Georgia 30356
R.Turner@xxx.com • 770-555-1212

• Goal •

Obtain a position as a bookkeeper

• Skills •

Handle accounts payable and receivable
Keep ledger records
Assist with budget forecasting
Calculate payroll deductions
Prepare periodic statements
Produce invoices
Supervise annual inventory

• Experience •

Georgia State University, Atlanta, GA
Bookkeeper, Campus Booksellers, 2003 to Present

Henderson, Inc., Memphis, TN
Clerk, Finance Department, Summers 2003 and 2004

• Education •

Georgia State University, Atlanta, GA
B.S. in Finance
Expected: May 2005

• References •

Available on request

Lawrence Oates

102 Maple Street
Louisville, KY 40201
Larry.Oates@xxx.com
502-555-4792

Career Goal

A technical position in the field of Electrical Engineering.

Education

University of Louisville, Louisville, KY
B.S., Electrical Engineering
Expected June 2004
GPA 3.56

Skills

Experience with DPL and Pascal.
Use of Unix, Wylbur, and Executive Operating Systems.
Knowledge of SPICE.

Work Experience

Nichols Technical, Inc., Memphis, TN
Technical Assistant, Summer 2003
Handled warehouse inspections, trend analyses, and programming.
Involved with statistics and parts engineering groups.

Activities

EE Club
President, Delta Upsilon Fraternity

References available upon request.

Mary E. Marlow

4455 West Gunderson Street
Berkeley, CA 94701
mary.marlow@xxx.com
Home: 415-555-4909
Pager: 415-555-6118

Goal

Labor and delivery staff R.N. position, with an opportunity to further develop neonatal intensive care skills.

Credentials

B.S.N., McAdams College, Berkeley, CA
California Nursing License #975-987436
C.P.R. and P.A.L.S. Certified
Member, California Nursing Association

Experience

Labor and Delivery Staff Nurse, 2003 to Present
Stevenson's Women's Hospital, Berkeley, CA
- Evaluate and triage patients upon admission.
- Monitor patients' progress.
- Teach self-care, pain management techniques, breastfeeding, and infant care.
- Care for healthy newborns in nursery.
- Arrange discharge planning.

Additional Information

References available.

Willing to relocate.

Anna Castillo

4742 N. Lawndale • Chicago, IL 60625
E-mail: anna.castillo@xxx.com • Pager: 312-555-2574

Objective   Children's Caseworker

Education   University of Illinois, Champaign, IL
Bachelor of Science, June 2003
Major: Social Work
Minor: Psychology

Work Experience   Association House, Chicago, IL
Case Manager, August 2003 to Present
• Provide social services to children, parents, and foster parents.
• Write case reports.

Memberships   Illinois Association of Social Workers
National Caseworkers Association

References   Submitted upon request

HAROLD C. JONES

609 Lincoln Road
Houston, Texas 77050
Home: 713-555-1947
E-mail: h.jones@xxx.com
Website: www.haroldjones.com

OBJECTIVE

Computer Programming Position

EDUCATION

Baylor University
B.S. in Computer Science
Completed June 2004
- Courses in COBOL, HTML, JavaScript, ADO, Database Management
- GPA of 3.9/4.0
- Earned 50% of tuition by working while carrying a full course load.

EMPLOYMENT

Computer Lab Assistant, 2002 to Present
Baylor University
- Instruct undergraduates in the use of computer hardware and software.
- Provide assistance ranging from word-processing instruction to programming assignments.

Sales Associate, Summers 2002 and 2003
Computer World
- Sold computer equipment and software.
- Answered customers' questions.
- Provided ongoing customer service and training.

References available upon request

Cristina Fernandez

7 S. Industrial Parkway
Hilo, HI 96721
C.Fernandez@xxx.com
808-555-8032

Education	M.B.A. in Marketing University of Hawaii, Hilo, HI Degree awarded June 2004 B.S. in Finance University of Colorado, Boulder, CO Degree awarded May 2002
Courses	Sales & Marketing Tax Law Business Law Consumer Behavior Mass Marketing Mass Communications Calculus Advertising Sales Management Statistics
Honors	Summa Cum Laude, 2002 Dean's List, 2001 and 2002
Work History	PACIFIC DEVELOPMENT CORPORATION Hilo, Hawaii Administrative Assistant, Sales Office August 2003 to Present • Handle billing, inventory, public relations, and correspondence. Sales Trainee Summer 2003 • Assisted with billing, orders, shipping, and inventory.
References	Available upon request

James Robert Weitsma

1200 Woodland Drive, #3E
Chicago, IL 60607

E-mail: jim.weitsma@xxx.com
Telephone: 312-555-4903

Objective

A position as a sales management trainee.

Education

Northwestern University, Evanston, IL
B.A. in Advertising, expected June 2005
Dean's List five quarters
3.6 GPA in major field
3.5 GPA overall

Activities

Alumni Committee
Student Activities Board

Work Experience

AT&T, Chicago, IL
Sales Intern, September 2004 to Present
Assist sales manager in areas of promotion, product development, and marketing.

Handleman Marketing, Winnetka, IL
Telephone Surveyor, Summer 2003

Yesterday's, Evanston, IL
Waiter, Summer 2002

Special Skills

Fluent in Spanish.
Familiar with Microsoft Office Suite, including Word, Excel, Access, and PowerPoint.

References available on request.

Robert LaPort

339 S. Jordan St.
Shreveport, LA 71101
Bob.LaPort@xxx.com
318-555-3893

Objective: A career in environmental testing.

Education: M.S. in Atmospheric Science, 6/03
                      North Carolina State University
                      Raleigh, NC

                      B.S. in Chemistry, 6/01
                      Shreveport College
                      Shreveport, LA

Experience: Wexler Corporation, Shreveport, LA
                      Position: Lab Chemist
                      Dates: 8/03 to Present
                      Duties: Analysis of chemical content in building
                      materials to comply with OSHA regulations.

                      North Carolina State University, Raleigh, NC
                      Position: Research Assistant
                      Dates: 9/02 to 6/03
                      Duties: Dispersion modeling of fugitive process
                      emissions from manufacturing operations such as
                      plastic pipe extrusion and injection molding.

References: Available upon request.

Sam Garrison
83 Main Place, #3B • Portland, ME 04129
S.Garrison@xxx.com • 207-555-2321

Objective
A position as an advertising assistant where I can use my advertising, marketing, and graphic arts skills.

Education
University of Maine, New Brunswick, ME
B.A. in Advertising, expected June 2004
Major Fields: Advertising, Marketing, Graphic Arts, Journalism, and Business

Honors
Dean's List
Worthington Academic Merit Scholarship

Work Experience
Lee J. Harris, Inc., Bangor, ME
Advertising Intern, Summer 2003
- Handled four accounts for advertising agency.
- Designed and laid out ads.
- Wrote copy for ads.
- Assisted with traffic control.
- Served as intermediary between client and account executives.

Bangor Life Magazine, Bangor, ME
Advertising Assistant, part-time, 2002
- Assisted in designing ads for magazine copy.
- Gained experience with Adobe Illustrator and Adobe Photoshop programs.
- Provided basic pricing and design information to clients.

New Brunswick Daily, New Brunswick, ME
Freelance writer, 2000 to 2002
- Wrote feature articles on local community news, including education, sports, politics, and the arts.
- Provided photos and illustrations in support of various articles.

References and portfolio are available upon request.

Sondra Jackson
1500 W. Redwood Dr.
Salt Lake City, UT 84110
801-555-3921
s.jackson@xxx.com

Overview
- Strong computer and organizational skills with an extensive knowledge of the travel industry
- Enjoy fast-paced work environment
- Excellent interpersonal and communications skills
- Interested in full-time travel agent position

Education
Salt Lake Community College
Certified Travel Agent, September 2003

Central High School
Diploma Awarded, May 2003

Experience
Harper Street Travel Agency
Part-Time Reservationist
July 2003 to Present

Skills
- Knowledge of Word, Access, and Excel
- Fluent in Spanish
- Typing speed of 60 words per minute

References Available

William Gavin

2666 Western Avenue, Apt. 44
Madison, WI 53703
B.Gavin@xxx.com
414-555-2029

Career Goal
A position with Parker Thomas Accounting as an accountant

Education
University of Wisconsin, Madison, WI
M.B.A. in Accounting, June 2003

University of Chicago, Chicago, IL
B.A. in Accounting, May 2001
• Triton Honorary Society
• Leopold Scholarship

Areas of Study
• Basic, Intermediate, and Advanced Accounting
• Business Law
• Cost Accounting
• Statistical Methods
• Planning and Control
• Tax Law
• Investments

Work History
Wisconsin Federal, Madison, WI
Trainee Examiner, 2003 to Present
• Participate in test audits, preparation of schedules of earnings, audits
  of expenses and capital accounts, and classification and appraisal
  of assets.

References available

Luis Castillo

8155 N. Knox
Skokie, IL 60076
L.Castillo@xxx.com
708-555-3168

Job Objective

Sales position where I can utilize my retail sales, cash management, and supervisory skills.

Work Experience

Gateway, Inc., Chicago, IL
Manager/Salesperson, 11/02–Present
Manage own jewelry business.
Sell jewelry at wholesale and retail levels.
Negotiate prices with customers.
Handle all finances and bookkeeping.

West Miami Jewelry, Miami, FL
Manager, 1/99–11/02
Managed a retail jewelry store.
Oversaw all aspects of sales, purchasing, and bookkeeping.
Supervised two employees.

Education

Interamerica Business Institute, Chicago, IL, 9/03–Present
Major: Business Management

Northeastern University, Chicago, IL
Attended 8/97–5/99
Area of concentration: Business Management

References available on request.

Maura Tresvant

33 N. Main St. • Fargo, ND 58102 • (701) 555-7310 • M.Tresvant@xxx.com

Goal

To obtain a position as a Legal Assistant for
a medium- to large-sized law firm.

Education

Stevenson College, Fargo, ND
A.A. degree, expected June 2004
Major: Legal Assisting Technology

Course Work

Tort and Insurance Law and Claims Investigation
Contracts, Sales, and Secured Transactions
Landlord and Tenant Mediation
Law Office Practice and Procedure
Wills and Trusts

Employment History

Prudential Insurance Company, Fargo, ND
Office Assistant, September 2003 - Present
Complete all general office duties
Assemble and transcribe dictation for sales staff
Handle typing, filing, and answering phones

Barker Company, Fargo, ND
Secretary, June 2002 - September 2003
Provided information to customers
Answered phones
Typed and processed orders

References on Request

William Perris

606 W. Washington, #1B

Chicago, IL 60657

b.perris@xxx.com

(312) 555-1201

Education

Roosevelt University, Chicago, IL
B.A. in Accounting, June 2004

Experience

City of Chicago, Chicago, IL
Finance Assistant, Department of Housing
Summer 2003
- Evaluated accounts and operations for compliance with department procedures and policies
- Assembled charts and tables
- Examined fiscal records and operating procedures
- Prepared audit reports

McCauley, Inc., Indianapolis, IN
Assistant, Accounting Department
Summer 2002
- Maintained books of original entry, trial balance, and general ledger
- Prepared financial statements
- Assisted with bank transactions, settlements, and adjustments

References furnished upon request

Barry Scrant

111 Willoughby Road, Apt. 3
Pierre, SD 57501
B.Scrant@xxx.com
(605) 555-2212

Objective

A job in personnel administration leading to personnel management.

Education

Jefferson University, Parkview, SD
B.A. in Sociology, expected June 2004
Areas of concentration: employee relations, psychology, communications

Skills and Experience

Interviewed 50 South Dakota farmers for senior research project, *The South Dakota Farm Industry: Boom or Bust?* Collected and analyzed data. Developed questionnaire.

Served as a student representative on the university's planning committee. Worked on a subcommittee that dealt with policy formulation.

Wrote the article "South Dakota's Future" for *South Dakota News*, October 1996.

Collected and analyzed statistical data on local Farm Union elections.

References

Provided on request.

➢ *Emmy Danokowski*

1600 Roberts Street
Andover, MA 01810
E.Danokowski@xxx.com
(415) 555-4155

➢ *Career Objective*

A position as an insurance underwriter

➢ *Education*

Parker College, Andover, MA
B.S. in Marketing, June 2003

➢ *Honors*

GPA 3.5
Harrison McDonald Scholarship Winner
Voted Outstanding Senior by Marketing Department

➢ *Work Experience*

E. Katsulos Associates, Andover, MA
2003–Present
Accomplishments:
Hired as junior insurance investigator and promoted to assistant claims representative within six months
Voted Employee of the Month in September 2003
Received favorable evaluation and was commended for discovering fraudulent health-care claims through investigation in the field

➢ *References*

Provided on request

Maria LaPenna

4390 S. Finley Rd.
Baton Rouge, LA 70802
504/555-3903
m.lapenna@xxx.com

Objective   A position utilizing my graphic design experience and education.

Education   University of Louisiana, Baton Rouge, LA
B.A. in Commercial Art, expected June 2005

Familiar with Macromedia Studio MX (Flash, Freehand, Cold Fusion, Fire Works) and Adobe Creative Suite (Photoshop, PageMaker, Illustrator, Premier, After Effects).

Experience   Baton Graphics, Baton Rouge, LA
Intern, Summer 2004

University of Louisiana, Baton Rouge, LA
Yearbook Art Director, 2002-2003

Emerge Magazine
Visual Art Editor, 2001

Membership   Art Directors and Artists Club, 2002 to Present

Award   University of Louisiana Student Design Competition
First Place, May 2002

References   Personal web page with design samples can be viewed at www.marialapenna.com.

References and portfolio available upon request.

Gavin T. Simpkins   **222 Handlebar Avenue**
                             Amarillo, TX 79118
                             (806) 555-8280

Objective: Machinist

Education: Amarillo Technical College, Amarillo, TX
                             A.S. Degree in Machine Shop, June 2003

Course Work: C.A.D. (Computer Aided Design)
                             Machine Shop
                             Fundamentals of Metallurgy
                             Drafting
                             Basics of Manufacturing
                             Technical Math
                             Welding
                             Introduction to Numerical Control

Skills: Drill Presses, Lathes, Grinding, and Mills

Work Experience: Fargo Packing Co., Plainview, TX
                             Maintenance Worker, 2002 - 2003
                             • Handled maintenance of company vehicles
                               and heavy machinery
                             • Parked and operated company trucks

References: Available on request

Tawana Johnson

1750 N. Normandie Ave.
Miami, FL 33239
Home: 305-555-2922
Office: 305-555-4000

Objective

A position at a commercial radio station.

Skills and Accomplishments

- Assisted in the management of a college radio station.
- Helped to direct and supervise staff.
- Established music format guidelines.
- Wrote and edited budget proposals.
- Assisted in budget decisions.
- Created and implemented new music format.
- Served as on-air personality.
- Trained a staff of disc jockeys.

Employment History

WLVE-Radio, Ft. Lauderdale, FL
Assistant General Manager, 2003–Present

WWOP-TV, New York, NY
Student Intern, Summer 2001

Education

University of South Florida, Ft. Lauderdale, FL
B.A. in Broadcasting, June 2003

Ft. Myers College, Ft. Myers, FL 1999–2001

References

Available upon request.

• **Mary Lynn Bademacher** •

250 North Brady Street
Cleveland, OH 44113
216-555-6906

• **Background**

Recently licensed electrician seeking a full-time position doing commercial, industrial, or residential electrical work.

• **Credentials**

Ohio License #C-57488
Certified by Cleveland Technical College Apprenticeship Program, June 2003

• **Employer**

DiAngelo Company
June 2003 to Present
• Responsible for a variety of commercial and industrial wiring projects.
• Interact with architects, contractors, and building inspectors.
• Have an excellent record of completing projects at or below projected costs, while complying with codes and meeting deadlines.

• **References**

Michael DiAngelo, Owner
DiAngelo Company
(216) 555-6958 Ext. 399

Eliza Sullivan, Director
Cleveland Technical College Apprenticeship Program
(216) 555-3932

RENEE C. CALDWELL
6500 RIVERSIDE DRIVE, APT. 422
WASHINGTON, DC 20010
R.CALDWELL@XXX.COM
202-555-5594

OBJECTIVE

Administrative Assistant

EDUCATION

Jefferson City College, Washington, DC
A.A. Office Administration and Technology
Date of Graduation: June 2003

SKILLS

Knowledge of Word, Access, and Excel
Familiar with GELCO accounting program
Typing speed of 65 words per minute
Excellent written and oral communication skills

EXPERIENCE

Adley Manufacturing, Washington, DC
Administrative Assistant/Receptionist
June 2003 to Present
Manage switchboard and front desk for midsize manufacturing firm.
Duties include greeting clients, answering and routing all incoming
calls, and producing correspondence.

REFERENCES

Submitted on request

Miguel Fernandez

5320 Wilshire Blvd. • Los Angeles, CA 90069
(213) 555-9282 • m.fernandez2@xxx.com

Objective

Seeking a marketing position in the music industry.

Work Experience

Hit Productions, Los Angeles, CA
Public Relations/Marketing Assistant, 5/03–Present
• Assist P.R. director with all duties, including radio promotion and
  retail marketing.
• Coordinate radio and print interviews for artists.
• Perform all typing and filing.
• Answer multiple line phones.

KCLA Radio, Los Angeles, CA
Music Director, 6/02–5/03
• Selected music for student radio station.
• Oversaw daily operations of music library and programming
  department.
• Supervised staff of six volunteers.

Education

University of California–Los Angeles, Los Angeles, CA
B.A. in Arts Management, 5/03

Activities

• Phi Mu Alpha Music Fraternity, President
• Alpha Lambda Fraternity

Special Skills

• Working knowledge of Microsoft Word, PowerPoint, and Excel.
• Fluent in Spanish.
• Experience with focus groups and surveying.
• Familiar with all genres of music, including Classical, Latino, Rock,
  Alternative, World, Folk, and Dance/Techno.

References available upon request.

Shirley G. Browne

2552 Willowbrook Lane
Boulder, CO 80304
Shirley.Browne@xxx.com
(303) 555-4849

Goal
R.N. Position

Experience
Volunteer Nursing Assistant, 2002 to Present
Mercy Hospice
- Assist nursing staff in providing primary care to terminally ill patients.
- Monitor patients' status and vital signs and report to nursing supervisor.
- Provide grooming and bathing assistance and emotional support for patients.

Medical Records Clerk, 2000 to 2002
Bishop Hospital
- Recorded patient histories and insurance information.
- Maintained patient database.
- Gained extensive knowledge of medical terminology.

Education
Bishop Hospital School of Nursing
R.N. expected June 2004

Credentials
C.P.R. certified
Member, American Student Nurses Association

References
Available upon request

ADRIENNA DYSON
5 Oak Avenue, #2 • Crescent City, MO 60166
A.Dyson@xxx.com • (816) 555-8161

JOB OBJECTIVE
To obtain a position in early childhood education or day care.

EDUCATION
South Missouri State College, Springfield, MO
B.A. in Early Childhood Education, expected June 2004

COURSE WORK
Early Childhood Education
Psychology of Learning
History of Childhood Problems
The Urban Family
The Exceptional Child

WORK HISTORY
South Missouri State College, Springfield, MO
Day Care Director, 2001 to Present
- Supervise day care services for the children of faculty members.
- Interview, select, and oversee student workers.
- Administer medicines and monitor all special needs for individual children.

Southmall Day Care, Springfield, IL
Teacher's Assistant, 1998 to 2000
- Assisted with play sessions, outdoor activities, and learning games.
- Met with parents regarding their child's progress.
- Monitored all aspects of children's day.
- Assisted with snack and nap times.

References provided on request.

Carol Page

500 E. Maple Street, Apt. #4
Eugene, OR 97412
Carol.Page@xxx.com
(503) 555-4122

Career Objective

To obtain a position as a librarian with the city of Seattle.

Education

University of Oregon, Eugene, OR
M.S. in Library Science
Degree expected June 2004

University of Mississippi, Oxford, MS
B.S. in Linguistics, May 2002

Work Experience

Eugene Public Library, Eugene, OR
Internship, 2002–2003
- Conducted research.
- Maintained and updated files.
- Assisted in the acquisition of new books.
- Organized and stocked audiovisual materials.

Oxford Public Library, Oxford, MS
Assistant to Children's Librarian, 2000–2001
- Developed reading programs for grade school children.
- Taught children the use of reference section and computer catalog.
- Acquired new books and magazines.

References available upon request.

Elizabeth O'Shea

233 Sandpiper Road • Cellular: (213) 555-9906
Los Angeles, CA 90012 • Home: (213) 555-3284

Goal
A career as a floral designer.

Education
Los Angeles City College, Los Angeles, CA
Certificate of Completion, June 2003
Ornamental Horticulture Program

Skills
- Floral Design: excellent understanding of floral arranging, plant care, and selection.
- Sales: experience with diverse customer base including corporate clients.
- Cash Management Skills: comfortable operating cash register and doing light bookkeeping.
- Marketing: familiar with marketing strategies to increase sales.

Work History
Freelance Floral Designer, 2003 to Present
- Design and sell dried floral arrangements for special occasions, especially weddings.
- Specialize in large arrangements and bridal bouquets.
- Purchase materials, create arrangements, and personally deliver all items.

Accomplishments
Increased business by 20 percent during the last year.
Initiated cooperative marketing arrangement with two area photographers and a caterer that has led to an increase in business for all participants.
Recently featured in *LA Living* magazine.

References available upon request.

Joann Bianchi
7282 56th Street
Richmond, CA 94530
J.Bianchi@xxx.com
(415) 555-8083

Objective

Personnel Management

Work Experience

Avery Publishing Company, San Francisco, CA
Payroll Specialist, 2002 - present
- Determine job-grading system.
- Evaluate jobs.
- Maintain employee budget.
- Conduct performance appraisals.
- Decide wage increases and adjustments.
- Set salary ranges.
- Write job descriptions.
- Coordinate compensation surveys.
- Gather data on vacations, sick time, and leaves of absence.

Education

University of California at Santa Barbara
Bachelor's Degree in Economics, May 2002

Personnel Management Institute
Harrison University, Seattle, WA
Summer 2002

Honors

UCSB Economics Scholarship, 2000 - 2002

Gamma Kappa Phi Honorary Society, 2000 - 2002

References

Available upon request

Marek Woriskowski
1711 North Logan Avenue • Atlantic City, NJ 08404
Home: (609) 555-4438 • Cellular: (609) 555-8971

Career Objective: A position in restaurant management utilizing my
                         food service experience and educational background.

Experience: **Food Service**
                         • Supervised kitchen staff of eight.
                         • Conducted business with a local catering service.
                         • Interviewed, hired, and trained student food ser-
                           vice workers.
                         • Catered banquets.
                         • Served dining patrons as a waiter.

                         Management
                         • Planned budget and strictly adhered to it.
                         • Organized work schedules for student workers.
                         • Managed purchasing, bookkeeping, and payroll.

                         Food Preparation
                         • Assisted in the preparation of meals for 90 chil-
                           dren and adults at a summer camp.
                         • Planned meals for 250 students.

Employment History: Szabo Food Service
                         Jersey College, Atlantic City, NJ
                         Food Service Director, 2003-present

                         Jersey College, Atlantic City, NJ
                         Assistant Cafeteria Director, 2002-2003

                         North Shore Children's Camp, Skokie, IL
                         Dining Hall Director, Summers 2001, 2002

                         Paco's Restaurant, Atlantic City, NJ
                         Waiter, 2000

Education: Jersey College, Atlantic City, NJ
                         B.S. in Business, expected June 2004

YOORI MATSUKA
Professional Respiratory Therapist

2100 West Harrison, Apt. 306
Chicago, IL 60633
y.matsuka@xxx.com
(312) 555-4849

SKILLS
Respiratory Therapy
Pulmonary Function Studies
EKG Testing
Stress Testing
CPR Instruction
Patient Education

WORK HISTORY
St. Jude's Medical Center, 2003 to Present
Respiratory Therapy Technician

Red Cross, 2002 to Present
Part-Time CPR Instructor

EDUCATION
New Haven Junior College, December 2002
Associate's Degree, Respiratory Therapy

REFERENCES
Available on request

Marvin Wilson

1444 Tyrone Avenue
Omaha, NE 68103
M.Wilson@xxx.com
(402) 555-3210

Objective

A career in business management.

Education

University of Nebraska, Omaha, NE
M.B.A. expected 6/04
Area of Concentration: Financial Management/Accounting

Shreveport College, Shreveport, LA
B.A. received 6/02
Major: Economics
Minor: Political Science

Work History

University of Nebraska, Omaha, NE
Analytical Studies Intern, 8/03 to Present
• Collect and organize data for university finance studies.
• Conduct library and online research.
• Edit final drafts of reports.

Shreveport College, Shreveport, LA
Resident Hall Assistant, 9/01 to 6/02
• Oversaw all aspects of college dormitory.
• Supervised resident, kitchen, and maintenance staff.
• Served as a liaison to the Student Affairs Office.

References

On Request.

Fred Schneider

9332 Hollywood Avenue • Camden, NJ 08630

F.Schneider@xxx.com • (609) 555-9599

Objective

Attorney

Education

Philadelphia College, Philadelphia, PA
Juris Doctor, June 2004

Tulane University, New Orleans, LA
Bachelor of Arts, June 2001
Major: English Literature

Course Work

Contracts
Criminal Law
Wills and Trusts
Juvenile Law
Trial Practice
Corporate Law
Family Law
Tax Law
Insurance Law
Legal Research

Activities & Honors

Bently Scholarship
Junior Bar Association
Dean's List
Student Government Representative
Planning Committee
Baseball Team

References

Available upon request

• Edward G. Williams •

4114 Sergeant Street, #3A
Cincinnati, OH 45217
E.Williams34@xxx.com
(513) 555-1129

• Objective

A career in the field of accounting

• Education

Cincinnati University, Cincinnati, OH
M.B.A., June 2002
Areas of Concentration: Accounting, Finance

University of Wisconsin, Madison, WI
B.A. in Political Science, 2000
Received Morgan Scholarship

• Employment

Barton & Morris, June 2002 to Present
Junior Public Accountant
- Assist public accounting staff in conducting audits for clients.
- Review financial records and reports to judge their accuracy.
- Suggest management control procedures to enable clients to function efficiently and economically.
- Provide timely, accurate data to assist clients with sales and merger decisions.

• Additional Information

- Received C.P.A. April 2003
- Currently studying for Certified Internal Auditor Exam
- Member, National Society of Public Accountants

• References

Available upon request.

Rorey Jeter

777 Yorba Linda Avenue • Jacksonville, FL 32222
r.jeter@xxx.com • (904) 555-6164

Goal:

A position in manufacturing with opportunities for advancement

Education:

Parker Institute of Technology, Jacksonville, FL
Bachelor of Science in Manufacturing Engineering Technology
Expected: June 2004

Selected Course Work
Work Measurement
Statistics
Manufacturing Analysis
Strength of Materials
Machine Design
Motion Analysis
Control Systems
Quality Assurance
Technical Writing
Planning

Employment History:

Florida Manufacturing Co., Tampa, FL
Forklift Driver, Summers 2002, 2003
Drove forklifts.
Repaired and serviced heavy machinery.

Penner Furniture, Inc., Panama City, FL
Warehouse Assistant, 1997-1999
Prepared furniture for delivery.
Organized furniture stock.
Delivered furniture.
Assisted in construction of furniture racks.

Membership:

Society of Manufacturing Engineers

References:

Submitted on request

James Shu

55 Stadium Drive   Home: 616-555-5600
Kalamazoo, MI 49048   Cellular: 616-555-8818

Career Goal: A position as a Medical Assistant

Education: Henderson Community College, Kalamazoo, MI
                        Medical Assistant Program
                        Certificate expected, June 2004

Experience: **Union Hospital, Kalamazoo, MI**
                        Internship, August 2003 to Present
                        • Assist with medical exams and minor surgery.
                        • Handle routine lab procedures.
                        • Interview and schedule patients.
                        • Prepare patients for examination and x-rays.
                        • Sterilize instruments.
                        • Organize and maintain medical records.

Membership: American Association of Medical Assistants

References: Submitted upon request

Janis Darien

345 West 3rd Street, Apt. 42

Boston, MA 02210

j.darien@xxx.com

(617) 555-3291

Job Objective
To obtain a position as a marketing management trainee.

Education
Boston University, Boston, MA
B.A. degree in Economics, June 2003
•Dean's List, four quarters
•3.5 GPA in major field, 3.8 GPA overall
•Plan to pursue graduate studies toward a Master's degree in Marketing at Boston University, Evening Division.

Work Experience
Lewis Advertising Agency, Boston, MA
Marketing Assistant, September 2003 to Present
•Assist Marketing Manager in areas of promotion, product development, and demographic analysis.

Paterno Marketing, Boston, MA
Telephone Interviewer, Summer 2002
•Conducted telemarketing surveys to help clients analyze demographics and product demand and to create marketing strategies.

Special Skills
•Fluent in French.
•Familiar with Word, Excel, and PowerPoint.
•Knowledge of a variety of online research resources.

References
Available on request.

CAMERON MARKS

418 Whitesburg Street
Wauconda, IL 60084
847-555-4949

OBJECTIVE: Nurse Assistant position

OVERVIEW: Nurse Assistant experience working with geri-
atric clients in long-term care setting.

- Monitor and record clients' vital signs, mood, and appearance.
- Assist nursing staff in meeting clients' basic grooming, bathing, and nutrition needs.
- Take direction well while also advocating for patients as needed.
- Provide information and emotional support to clients and their families.
- Participate in care management conferences.
- Cooperate with nursing, physical therapy, and respiratory therapy personnel to develop comprehensive client care plans.

Prior experience in a pediatric office setting.

- Scheduled appointments and greeted patients.
- Handled office phones, files, and correspondence.

EMPLOYERS: Pinkerton Nursing Center, Wauconda, IL
Nurse Assistant, 6/03 to Present

Kusler Medical Group, Deerfield, IL
Office Assistant, 4/01 to 6/03

EDUCATION: Nurse Assistant Certification, 6/03
Columbia College, Chicago, IL

REFERENCES: Available

♥ Kids Inc. ♥

Quality Day Care ♥ *Affordable Rates* ♥ *Flexible Hours*
Excellent References

Serita Thomas

75 Crescent Lane   Birmingham, AL 35233   205-555-5059
www.kidsinc.com

Credentials

Alabama State University, Birmingham, AL
B.A. in Early Childhood Education
Minor: Psychology
Graduated June 1997

Courses

Psychology of Learning
Early Childhood Education
History of Childhood
The Urban Family
The Exceptional Child

Work History

June 2002 to Present
Owner/Operator, Kids Inc. Day Care
- Provide quality day care from my home.
- Offer full-time, part-time, and drop-in services.
- Provide a safe and stimulating atmosphere for preschool children.

June 1997 to June 2002
Stay-at-home mother
- Provided care for my two children.
- Managed all household duties including meal preparation and family budgeting.

May 1995 to June 1997
Teacher's Assistant, Birmingham University Day Care
- Assisted director of university day care center in providing games and learning activities for children of faculty and staff.

References available upon request.

William Harris

P.O. Box 4112
Fargo, ND 58109
will.harris@xxx.com
(701) 555-3930

Objective: To obtain an entry-level position at a commercial radio
station.

Radio Experience: WND-Radio, Fargo, ND
Assistant to the General Manager, 2003–2004
- Assisted in the management of a student-run col-
lege radio station.
- Helped to direct and supervise a board of directors
and an on-air staff to ensure efficient day-to-day
operations.
- Established music format guidelines and made
other management decisions.
- Wrote and edited budget proposals.
- Assisted in financial matters.

WND-Radio, Fargo, ND
Alternative Music Director, 2000–2003
- Created and implemented station's alternative
music format.
- Worked with a staff of 15 on-air disc jockeys.
- Planned and organized club performances by local
bands in conjunction with the station.
- Served as on-air personality.

Education: Fargo College, Fargo, ND
B.S. in Business Administration, June 2004
Minor: Music

Activities: Studio Engineer, 2001–2002
News Announcer, 2002
Treasurer, Glee Club, 2001–2002
Football Team, 2001–2003

References: Provided on request.

LISA MOEN

1433 Eagleton Avenue
Charlotte, NC 28210
L.Moen@xxx.com
(704) 555-5565

Job Sought

A career in the field of juvenile justice.

Education

University of North Carolina, Charlotte, NC
Bachelor of Social Work, expected May 2004

Honors

Mecklenburg County Medical Society Scholarship
Dean's List, three semesters

Employment History

UNC, Charlotte, NC
Department Assistant, 2002 to Present
• Assist students with department materials and coordinate academic
  counseling sessions.
• Oversee interviewing and hiring of student workers.

Angels Hospital, Brooklyn, NY
Volunteer, Summers 2001 and 2002
• Participated in various programs in the youth activity area.
• Helped organize community outreach clinic for at-risk youths.

References

Available upon request.

Trevor Maine

707 17th Street
Harrisburg, PA 17109
T.Maine@xxx.com
(717) 555-1689

Education
Pennsylvania State University, Harrisburg, PA
B.S. in Biotechnology, expected June 2004
• GPA 3.36
• Dean's List

Courses
Evolution, Biodiversity, and Environment
Science and Technology Studies
Principles of Biochemistry
Applied Cell and Molecular Biology
Ecology and Evolutionary Physiology
From Molecular Genetics to Biotechnology
Bioethics

Work Experience
Environmental Protection Agency, Harrisburg, PA
Associate Field Researcher, 2003–Present
• Assist with gathering data through water and soil sampling.
• Develop ecosystem-level models for testing water quality.

Computer Skills
Microsoft Word, Access, and PowerPoint
Experienced with online research
Familiar with numerous molecular biology programs

Honors
Dean's List
Biology Honor Society

References
Available on request

Kadira Causevic

432 Sentinel Avenue • Kansas City, MO 64109
K.Causevic152@xxx.com • (816) 555-3903

Objective: A career in advertising media services.

Education: Stevens College, Kansas City, MO
B.A. in Advertising, expected June 2004
• 3.66 GPA in major field
• Student Government Secretary
• Homecoming Committee
• Plan to pursue a Master's degree at a future date.

Work Experience: Anders Publishing, Inc., Kansas City, MO
Marketing Intern, Summer 2003
• Assisted Marketing Manager of book publisher.
• Helped produce book catalog and develop pricing and marketing strategies.
• Tracked and analyzed sales of selected titles.
• Prepared sales analysis for management use.

Survey Service, Inc., Kansas City, MO
Telephone Surveyor, Summers 2001 and 2002

Radical Records, East Lydon, MO
Salesperson, Summer 2000

Special Skills: • Working knowledge of German, French, and Spanish.
• Familiar with Word, Photoshop, and Power Point programs.
• Typing speed of 65 wpm.
• Knowledge of customized databases, including ADMARC.

References: Available on request.

Tracy Vanderlee

404 East Emerald Street
Portland, ME 04107
T.Vanderlee@xxx.com
(207) 555-5579

Goal

To further pursue my career in finance.

Achievements

Dispersed funds for student groups and activities.
Designed operating budget for student government.
Handled accounts payable and receivable.
Approved financial reports.
Served as co-chair of Budget Approval Committee.
Oversaw deposits and withdrawals for customer accounts.
Processed traveler's checks, cashier's checks, and money orders.

Work Experience

Teller, June 2003 to Present
First Bank, Portland, Maine

Student Government Treasurer, September 2002 to June 2003
Portland College, Portland, ME

Education

Portland College, Portland, ME
B.S. in Business, June 2003
Minor in Accounting

References

Available on request.

MICHELLE CRUMLEY

2316 Sherman Avenue, Apt. 3B • Evanston, IL 60201
M.Crumley@xxx.com • (847) 555-4727

EDUCATION
Northwestern University, Evanston, IL
B.S. in Journalism
Expected June 2004
GPA of 3.6

HONORS
Phi Beta Kappa
Dean's List - Seven Quarters
Owen L. Coon Award, Honorable Mention

ACTIVITIES
President, Activities and Organizations Board
Wa-Mu Show
Captain, Soccer Team
Freshman Advisor

WORK EXPERIENCE
Evanston Review, Evanston, IL
Intern, Summer 2003
• Assisted in layout, editing, and reporting for local newspaper.
• Wrote and edited articles.
• Handled preparatory research for local election coverage.

Northwestern University, Evanston, IL
Assistant to the Registrar, General Office, 2002 - 2003
• Processed transcript requests.
• Entered registrations into the computer.
• Provided information to students.

SPECIAL SKILLS
Knowledge of French and Russian.
Strong computer experience, including Wordstar software.
Comfortable with both PC and Mac computers.
Familiar with *The Chicago Manual of Style.*

REFERENCES
Available on request.

MARGARET LEONARDO
CERTIFIED LEGAL ASSISTANT

9991 E. Oak Dr., Apt. 14C • Los Angeles, CA 90029
M.Leonardo@xxx.com • (213) 555-1343

EDUCATION

California State University, Los Angeles, CA
Paralegal Program
Certificate of Completion, September 2004

University of California, Santa Barbara, CA
B.S. in English, May 2004
Summa Cum Laude

WORK EXPERIENCE

Oppenheim & Kensit, Los Angeles, CA
Intern January 2004–September 2004
• Drafted legal documents.
• Assisted in the preparation of cases for trial.
• Conducted legal research.
• Handled memoranda of law.

MEMBERSHIP

National Association of Legal Assistants

REFERENCES

Provided on request

Lisa Shapiro

7007 Catskills Avenue, Apt. 4 • Ithaca, NY 14852
Home: 607-555-4444 • Office: 607-555-2831
E-mail: Lisa.Shapiro@xxx.com

Objective:

Insurance Underwriter

Education:

Ithaca College, Ithaca, NY
B.S. in Business Administration, May 2003
• Minor in Spanish
• Gergerheim Scholarship

Relevant Courses:

Principles of Insurance
Business Law
Tax Law
Business Risk Management
Accounting
Economics

Work History:

Johnson Insurance Co., Ithaca, NY
Junior Claims Representative, June 2003 to present
• Process routine insurance claims.
• Flag questionable claims and conduct preliminary investigation.
• Conduct significant phone contact with clients and health-care providers.
• Responsible for issuing monthly claims status report.

Davidson & Browne, Attorneys at Law
Parker Meadows, NY
Legal Assistant, September 2001 to May 2003
• Assisted attorneys part-time in handling insurance claims.
• Mastered legal terms related to insurance work.
• Responsible for typing, filing, and phones.
• Maintained databases.

References:

On request

TIMOTHY WARSHAWSKI

555 Kenneth Avenue   T.Warshawski@xxx.com
Baltimore, MD 21210   (410) 555-7020

GOAL: An entry-level position in an architecture
                   firm

EDUCATION: M.Arch June 2004
                   University of Maryland, Baltimore, MD

                   B.A. in English, 2002
                   University of Georgia, Atlanta, GA

COURSE WORK: History of Modern Architecture
                   Visual Communication
                   Introduction to Urban Planning
                   Theories of Urban Form
                   Design and Energy
                   Problems and Methods of Architectural
                       Preservation

FIELDWORK: Intern, 2004 to Present
                   Lehman Associates, Baltimore, MD

                   CADD Technician, 2002 to 2004
                   Perkins & Will, Baltimore, MD

REFERENCES: Available

Audrey West

5968 Princeton Road
Las Vegas, NV 89890
A.West@xxx.com
702-555-6979

Goal

Full-time position as magazine copy editor

Education

B.A. in English, June 2003
University of Southern California

Skills

Copyediting
Page layout experience
Photo editing experience
Knowledge of *AP Stylebook* and *The Chicago Manual of Style*
Familiar with Quark, PageMaker, Photoshop, and Illustrator

Experience

Copy Editor, *Southwest Magazine*, July 2003 to Present
- Copyedit features, check facts, and prepare all material for press.
- Assist in selection of photos and design of layouts.
- Work in fast-paced atmosphere and meet tight production deadlines.

Photo Editor, *USC News*, September 2002 to June 2003
- Selected photos for alumni magazine, designed layout, and proofed copy.
- Acted as a liaison between publication and freelance photographers.

References

Available

▌▌▌ *Calvin Browne*

2316 King Street
Richardson, TX 75080
c.browne@xxx.com
(972) 555-2552

▌ *Goal*
Petroleum engineering position with small, independent oil exploration and production company

▌ *Education*
University of Texas at Dallas
B.S. in Petroleum Engineering, expected May 2004

▌ *Course Work*
Petroleum Engineering Design
Rocks and Fluids
Reservoir Modeling
Reservoir Engineering
Secondary Recovery
Drilling Design and Production

▌ *Work Experience*
University of Texas at Dallas
Lab Assistant/Physics Department, 2002–2003
- Assisted professors in the Physics Department with lab experiments and general office work.

▌ *Memberships*
Society of Petroleum Engineers
Engineering Club

▌ *Special Skills*
Strong computer skills
Fluent in Spanish

References available upon request

▪ STEVEN MIKOVICH

589 Third Street
Bowling Green, KY 42104
Home: (270) 555-4900
Cellular: (270) 555-3901
Mikovich@xxx.com

EXPERTISE

- Corporate Identity Design
- Print Media Design
- Web Page Design

EDUCATION

Colorado State University, Denver, CO
Bachelor of Arts, June 2003

- Major: Visual Communications
- Minor: Computer Science
- Knowledge of all major design software, including PageMaker, Quark, Adobe Illustrator, Adobe Photoshop, Freehand, and Flash

WORK EXPERIENCE

Colorado State University, Denver, CO
Graphic Designer, University Publications Department
July 2003 to Present

- Develop design concepts, page layouts, and cover designs for university publications, including student yearbook, alumni directories, and academic journals.
- Use PageMaker and Adobe Illustrator programs extensively.

MEMBERSHIPS

- Art Directors of Denver
- American Design Council
- Delta Gamma Fraternity

REFERENCES

Provided upon request

DOUG WESTON

**1688 East 3rd Street • Houston, TX 77702 • D.Weston@xxx.com
(713) 555-5277**

Career Goal: To work as an attorney for a large law firm specializing in criminal law.

Bar Membership: Texas State Bar, November 2003

Employment: **Houston Public Defender's Office
Houston, TX
Law Clerk, 2002 to Present**
• Oversee minor crime investigations.
• Interview witnesses.
• Serve subpoenas.
• Prepare investigation reports.

**Nuhfer & Nuhfer, Houston, TX
Law Clerk, 2001 to 2002**
• Drafted pleadings.
• Performed field investigations.
• Researched case law.
• Took depositions.
• Prepared trial briefs.

**University of California, Irvine, CA
Student Assistant, Admissions Office
1997 to 2000**
• Led campus tours for prospective students.
• Processed applications.
• Assisted in student recruitment and general public relations activities.

Education: University of Houston, Houston, TX
Juris Doctor, May 2003
Class Rank: Top 10 percent

University of California, Irvine, CA
B.S. in Political Science, June 1999

Honors: Dean's List at the University of Houston, 2000 to 2003
Moot Court, National Competition
Texas Law Award

References: Submitted upon request.

David T. Sanchez

1001 W. Edina Ave.

Edina, MN 55436

d.sanchez@xxx.com

(612) 555-5453

Strengths

• Excellent communication and people skills
• Strong photographic and processing skills
• Academic and hands-on training in commercial art
• Computer literate, with working knowledge of Quark and PageMaker

Education

University of Minnesota, St. Paul, MN
B.A. in Commercial Art, expected May 2004

Work Experience

Minneapolis Magazine, Minneapolis, MN
Commercial Artist, Summers 2001 – present

University of Minnesota, St. Paul, MN
Designer, University Publications, 2003

University of Minnesota, St. Paul, MN
Photographer, *Student Gazette*, 2002–2003

Workshops

• Website Design Seminar, University of Minnesota, 2003
• Illustration Workshop, Art Institute of Chicago, 2002
• Midwest Design Seminar, Northern Illinois University, 2001

References

Available upon request

Stewart Cahl, C.L.A.

4201 N. Broadway
Lafayette, IN 47906
317-555-7498
SKCahl@xxx.com

Overview
- Graduated from paralegal training program at Roosevelt University.
- Ranked in top 10 percent of class.
- Received C.L.A. certification from National Association of Legal Assistants.
- Currently employed by small legal firm specializing in tax and corporate law.
- Seeking to use my skills in legal research and document preparation at large law firm where I may broaden my exposure to all areas of the law.

Experience
Draft legal documents
Conduct research
Attend hearings
Handle SEC filings
Compile case citations
Assist in preparing witnesses for depositions
Prepare cases for appeal

Employers
Simon, Robb & Hobbes, Lafayette, IN
Legal Assistant, July 2003 to present

Cohen & Cohen, Raleigh, NC
Office Assistant, May 2002 to June 2003

Education
Roosevelt University, Chicago, IL
Paralegal Training Program
Certificate, June 2003

North Carolina State University, Raleigh, NC
B.A. in Economics, June 2002

References
Available on request

Kevin Wong

5449 Magnolia Way, #4B
North Hollywood, CA 91601
K.Wong23@xxx.com
818-555-7344

Objective

To obtain a position as a production assistant.

Work Experience

Saber Productions, Burbank, CA
Production Assistant, June 2003 - present
• Assist television producer and production coordinator.
• Organize transportation for cast and crew members.
• Copy and distribute scripts.
• Assist location manager.

Feder Film Productions, San Francisco, CA
Production Coordinator, Summer 2002
• Scouted locations; acquired film permits and props.
• Handled airline reservations and accommodations for talent.
• Oversaw the distribution of press releases.
• Photographed promotional stills.
• Supervised extras.

Chicago Film Festival, Chicago, IL
Production Assistant, Summer 2001
• Helped produce and distribute promotional material.
• Assisted with the day-to-day operations of the film festival.

KBT Radio, University of Seattle, Seattle, WA
Producer, 2001 - 2003
• Served as an announcer on a weekly newscast.
• Edited copy for newscast.
• Investigated and reported on student events.
• Handled on-air coverage of local elections.
• Trained and supervised employees.

Education

University of Seattle, Seattle, WA
B.A. in Film Production, June 2003

Clarence Smith

600 West Porter Street
Las Vegas, NV 89890
Clarence.Smith@xxx.com
(702) 555-3893

Education
University of Nevada, Las Vegas, NV
Bachelor of Arts in Communications
Expected June 2004

Honors
Dean's List (four semesters)
Dornburn Academic Merit Scholarship
Excellence in Communications Award (given to outstanding student researcher)

Activities
President, Kappa Beta Fraternity
New Student Week Committee
Homecoming Planning Committee
Captain, Tennis Team

Work Experience
Port Rand & Associates, Seattle, WA
Advertising Intern, 2003

Assisted sales staff in the areas of research, demographics, sales forecasts, identifying new customers, and promotion.

Communications Department
University of Nevada, Las Vegas, NV
Research/Office Assistant, 2002-2003

Researched and compiled materials for department professors. Arranged filing system and supervisor's library. Organized department inventory.

References available upon request

DANIEL LUI

173 MAPLEWOOD ROAD
TERRE HAUTE, IN 47802
317-555-1337
DANIEL.LUI224@XXX.COM

OBJECTIVE	A position in the field of Electrical Engineering with an emphasis on aviation electronic systems.
EDUCATION	B.S. in Electrical Engineering, May 2005 Rose-Hulman Institute of Technology, Terre Haute, IN • GPA 3.75 • Graduated with Honors
WORK EXPERIENCE	**C & S Industrial Design Consultants, Richardson, TX** **Summer Intern, 2004** • Assisted in research and development department of aviation electronics firm. • Input data, typed performance specifications reports, calibrated lasers, and maintained test equipment. **Rose-Hulman Institute of Technology, Terre Haute, IN** **Assistant to the Director, Financial Aid, 2002–2004** • Processed applications. • Handled general office duties.
ACTIVITIES	President, Student Chapter of Institute of Electrical and Electronics Engineers Peer Advisor, Engineering Department
REFERENCES	Available upon request.

Patricia Ardinger

66 Chambers Road
Hartford, CT 06101
Pat.Ardinger@xxx.com
(203) 555-2229

Overview

- Seeking position as Spanish Teacher at the secondary level.
- Currently completing M.A. thesis project.
- Provisionally licensed to teach in the state of Connecticut.

Education

University of Hartford, West Hartford, CT
Master's Degree in Education, expected June 2005
4.0 GPA in major

Grinnell College, Grinnell, IA
Bachelor's Degree in Education, with a minor in
Spanish, May 2002

Experience

Central High School, Hartford, CT
Student Teacher, Spanish Department
January 2004 - Present
Supervisor: Kaye Brendt

University of Hartford, West Hartford, CT
Tutor, Writing Lab
September 2003 - December 2003

Grinnell College, Grinnell, IA
Teaching Assistant for Expository Writing Course
September 2001 - May 2002

Memberships

American Federation of Teachers
National Education Association
PTA

References

Submitted upon request.

Qeeri Tujamota   *Graphic Designer*

1290 West Forest Avenue   Tujamota@xxx.com
Milwaukee, WI 53223   www.tujamota.com
414-555-2029

Experience

Regis Advertising, Milwaukee, WI
Graphic Designer, 2002 to Present
- Develop and execute projects from initial design through completion of camera-ready art.

University of Illinois at Chicago
Graphic Designer, University Art Gallery, 2001-2002
- Designed posters and brochures to promote student art exhibits.

University of Illinois at Chicago
Graphic Designer, Media Center, 2000-2001
- Assisted faculty and staff with design concepts. Helped produce camera-ready art for special events, curriculum support, and distance learning projects.

Education

University of Illinois at Chicago
B.A. in Visual Communications, 2002

Software

- Macromedia Studio: Flash, Freehand, Cold Fusion, Fireworks, and Director
- Adobe CS: Photoshop, PageMaker, Illustrator, Premier, and After Effects
- Apache and PHP
- Quark

Memberships

Midwest Design Coalition
Women in Design

Awards

- Midwest Design Contest for Advertising Design, Honorable Mention, October 2003
- University of Illinois Art Show, Best in Show, June 2002

References available on request

<u>*George Pasterneck*</u>

1119 South Figueroa Avenue
Miami, FL 33303
G.Pasterneck@xxx.com
(305) 555-6766

Education

<u>University of Miami, Miami, FL</u>
Graduate School of Business Administration
M.B.A. expected, June 2004
- Concentration: Finance
- Finance Club
- Student Advisory Board

<u>Boston University, Boston, MA</u>
B.A. in Economics, 2002
- Summa Cum Laude
- Phi Beta Kappa
- Student Government Vice President

Work Experience

<u>Studebaker & Bostwick, Miami, FL</u>
Financial Accounting Intern
September 2003 to Present
- Participate in standard accounting, credit approval, budgeting, and variance analysis.
- Handle bank balances and money management.

<u>First Florida Bank, Ft. Lauderdale, FL</u>
Commercial Loan Intern
January 2003 to May 2003
- Oversaw accounts in the automated teller system.
- Provided financial data to commercial account officers.
- Handled the collection of arrears.

<u>Boston University, Boston, MA</u>
Assistant, Accounts Payable Department
September 2001 to December 2002
- Assisted with bookkeeping, check requests, and disbursements.
- Billed invoices.
- Tracked accounts receivable and accounts payable.

References

Available upon request

Alan Beltzman • • •

1171 Sherman Avenue
Evanston, IL 60202
A.Beltzman@xxx.com
847-555-2741

• Objective

Staff Writer/Researcher for the news department of a newspaper where I can use my editorial, writing, and reporting skills

• Education

Northwestern University, Evanston, IL
B.A. in Journalism and Political Science (Double Major)
Expected Graduation Date: June 2004

• Accomplishments

- Write regular column on political issues for campus newspaper
- Won journalism award for feature series on "The Nuclear Threat"
- Researched and wrote pamphlets for city council on crime, gentrification, and zoning
- Edited grant proposals for local theater company
- Served as assistant researcher for NBC opinion poll

• Employment History

The Daily Northwestern, Evanston, IL
Staff Writer, 2001 to Present

Evanston City Council, Evanston, IL
Researcher/Writer, 2002 to 2003

Victory Gardens Theater, Chicago, IL
Editor, 2002

NBC-TV, Chicago, IL
Researcher, 2002

• References

Available on request

TONJA WILLIAMS

1661 HAVERHILL DRIVE • CEDAR RAPIDS, IA 52411
T.WILLIAMS@XXX.COM • (319) 555-8888

JOB OBJECTIVE

Engineering Technician/Camera Operator

OVERVIEW

Experience with all camera operations for film and video. Skills
include studio lighting, set design, film editing, dubbing, gaffing,
audio-video switching, mixing, and technical troubleshooting.

EXPERIENCE

WCED-TV, Cedar Rapids, IA
Engineering Assistant, July 2002–present

Drawbridge Productions, Des Moines, IA
Assistant Camera Operator, Summer 2001

WWOR Radio, Jackson, MS
Engineer, September 2000–July 2001

EDUCATION

Jackson University, Jackson, MS
B.A. in Communication Arts, June 2002

REFERENCES

Available on request

TYRELL STEVENSON   602 South Texas Avenue • Oakland, CA 94608
t.stevenson@xxx.com • (415) 555-3168

Job Objective: A position in hotel management.

Education: International School of Business
San Francisco, CA
January 2003 - December 2004
Certificate, Hotel Management

World Travel Institute, Sacramento, CA
January 2000 - December 2000
Certificate, Travel Consultant

Eastern Illinois University, Charleston, IL
Attended 1996 - 1998
Area of concentration: Business Management

Work Experience: Reddraan, Inc., Oakland, CA
Manager/Sales Executive
November 2003 - present
• Manager and sales executive for cookware
  business.
• Sell cookware at wholesale and retail levels.
• Negotiate prices with customers.
• Handle all finances and bookkeeping.

Eastmont Hotel, Oakland, CA
Student Intern
January 2003 - June 2003
• Assisted Food and Beverage Manager for
  200-key hotel.
• Responsible for inventory management, data
  entry, and purchasing.

Westerly Travel, Chicago, IL
Travel Consultant
January 2001 - December 2002
• Sold airline tickets and tour packages.
• Advised customers on travel plans.
• Handled ARC reports to airline corporations.

References: Available on request.

Sample Cover Letters

This chapter contains sample cover letters for people who have recently completed their education, and who are pursuing a wide variety of jobs and careers.

There are many different styles of cover letters in terms of layout, level of formality, and presentation of information. These samples also represent people with varying amounts of education and work experience. Choose one cover letter or borrow elements from several different cover letters to help you construct your own.

DANIEL LUI

173 MAPLEWOOD ROAD
TERRE HAUTE, IN 47802
317-555-1337
DANIEL.LUI224@XXX.COM

August 21, 20--

Robert Crain
Director of Human Services
Farrallon, Inc.
787 East Fourier Drive
Emeryville, CA 94608

Dear Mr. Crain:

After your visit to Rose-Hulman last March, we spoke about opportunities within your company for Electrical Engineers. You indicated that new positions would be opening this fall. I am writing to request an interview for one of those openings.

In May, I graduated from Rose-Hulman with a B.S. in Electrical Engineering. I graduated with honors in the top 10 percent of my class. My course work included Microwave Circuit Design, Electromagnetic Waves, Digital Integrated Circuits, and Systems and Signals.

As I look forward to my career in this field, I know that I would be able to make good use of my education working for Farrallon. I have enclosed a copy of my resume and will call next week to discuss setting up an interview. If you have any questions, please feel free to contact me via the phone number or e-mail address listed above.

Sincerely,

Daniel Lui

Patricia Ardinger

66 Chambers Road
Hartford, CT 06101
Pat.Ardinger@xxx.com
(203) 555-2229

June 1, 20--

Ed Peters
Principal
East Ridge High School
7001 Woodridge Road
Hartford, CT 06152

Dear Mr. Peters:

I am responding to your advertisement in the *Hartford Gazette* for a Spanish teacher. As the enclosed resume indicates, I have the credentials you are seeking. I am eager to put my skills to work for East Ridge.

My background includes a B.A. in Education from Grinnell College with a minor in Spanish, and I am finishing my M.A. in Education at the University of Hartford. My student teaching experience includes two semesters teaching Spanish I and one semester supervising a discussion section of Spanish Literature at Central High School.

I would enjoy hearing more about the current opening and look forward to talking with you. Please contact me by phone at (203) 555-2229 between eight and ten o'clock a.m.

Thank you in advance for your time and consideration.

Sincerely,

Patricia Ardinger

Lori Wu

489 McCauley   Oakland, CA 94609
Lori.Wu@xxx.com   Home: (415) 555-7020   Pager: (415) 555-0026

August 8, 20--

Tanya Woods
Director of Personnel
Department of Children's Services
33 West 43rd Street
Oakland, CA 94990

Dear Ms. Woods:

As a recent graduate of Stanford University's Master of Social Work program, I am looking forward to a rewarding career providing social services to disadvantaged children. As an Oakland native, I feel a special affinity to this city and a unique desire to help make it a better place for our children to live. For these reasons, I am writing to acquire about current openings for a Children's Caseworker.

While at Stanford, my studies included Theory of Social Work, Urban Problems, Case Analysis, Abnormal Psychology, and Social Welfare Systems. My fieldwork includes positions as a counselor for Covenant House in Oakland, an interviewer for the Oakland Drug Rehab Program, and a volunteer for the San Francisco Youth Center.

I have enclosed my resume for your review. As you will see, my training and experience in the field have prepared me for a position in your agency. Please contact me if you would like to speak further regarding my education and experience in the social services field. Thank you in advance for your time and consideration.

Sincerely,

Lori Wu

Derek Miller

15 Nob Hill Street • San Francisco, CA 94105

E-mail: D.Miller@xxx.com • (415) 555-4389

January 3, 20--

Gilbert Fanter, President
Unicorn Designs, Inc.
2442 Market Street, Suite 4C
San Francisco, CA 94107

Dear Mr. Fanter:

Your art director, Robin White, recently informed me that Unicorn Designs is interested in hiring additional Graphic Designers. I am writing to introduce myself and to let you know of my interest in working for your firm as a Graphic Designer.

As the enclosed resume indicates, I am a recent graduate of the Berkeley College of Design, where I received a B.A. in Graphic Design. My areas of concentration included Photography, Publication Design, Copywriting, Typography, and Systems. I have worked as a Graphic Design Intern at Berkeley and as a Graphics Assistant at Fern Labs.

Now that I have earned my degree and gained the needed experience, I am ready for the challenge of a position at a company such as Unicorn. I would appreciate the opportunity to speak with you in person and present my portfolio. Please feel free to contact me via e-mail or phone at your convenience. I look forward to speaking with you soon.

Sincerely,

Derek Miller

Carol Page

500 E. Maple Street, Apt. #4
Eugene, OR 97412
Carol.Page@xxx.com
(503) 555-4122

October 3, 20--

Sarah Banks, Head Librarian
Seattle Public Library
5000 Lake Parkway
Seattle, WA 98188

Dear Ms. Banks:

I am applying for the position of Reference Librarian, which was posted in the Library Science Department at the University of Oregon.

I am attending the University of Oregon's Library Science program and expect to be graduated in June of 2004. I earned my undergraduate degree, a B.S. in Linguistics, from the University of Mississippi.

While attending school at the University of Oregon, I have interned at the Eugene Public Library and assisted the Children's Librarian at the Oxford Public Library. The skills and insights that I have gained from these opportunities have prepared me for a position as a Reference Librarian.

I have enclosed my resume and I think you will agree that my qualifications are a perfect fit for this position. I look forward to meeting you and discussing this position soon.

Sincerely,

Carol Page

May 15, 20--

Deborah Klugh
Director of Human Resources
ABC
11 Rockefeller Plaza
New York, NY 10020

Dear Ms. Klugh:

This letter is in response to your ad in the *New York Times* for a P.R. Assistant. Enclosed are my resume and salary requirements as requested.

Next month I will be graduating from Boston University with a degree in Communications and a concentration in Public Relations. I was inducted into Phi Beta Kappa this month and expect to graduate with honors in June.

I am interested in working in the television industry and would be most pleased to be a part of the ABC team. I possess strong written and verbal communication skills and feel certain that I would do an excellent job in meeting the demands of this position.

Please contact me if you are interested in speaking with me further. I am willing to travel to New York for an interview. Thank you for your time and consideration.

Sincerely,

Barton T. Quigley
Boston University
Fenton Hall, 199 West Hampshire Way
Boston, MA 02201
(617) 555-3839

May 3, 20--

Gary Pupka
President
American Finance Company
4444 East River Drive
Detroit, MI 48201

Dear Mr. Pupka:

As a recent graduate of The Kellogg School of Business Management at
Northwestern University, I am seeking a position in financial management. I recently met a representative of your company, Jonathan Siveva,
at a recruiting seminar at Northwestern, and he alerted me to the fact that
your company would be hiring M.B.A.s this upcoming summer.

At Kellogg, my concentration was in Finance and Administration. I was
also a member of the Finance Club and served as a member of the Student Advisory Board. My practical experience includes a financial
accounting internship at Thomas & Thomas, an internship in the commercial loan department at LaSalle National Bank, and a position in the
accounts payable department at Northwestern.

I am enclosing my resume to give you a more comprehensive picture of
my accomplishments and qualifications. I will contact you in the next
week to inquire about setting up an interview. Thank you in advance for
your time and consideration.

Sincerely,

Antonio Marino
3200 Lake Shore Drive, #442
Chicago, IL 60614
(773) 555-2939

William Gavin

2666 Western Avenue, Apt. 44
Madison, WI 53703
B.Gavin@xxx.com
414-555-2029

July 22, 20--

Neil Tennant
Director of Human Resources
Parker Thomas Accounting, Inc.
7717 East 3rd Terrace
Milwaukee, WI 53225

Mr. Tennant:

I am seeking employment in the field of accounting, particularly a position that might prepare me for management. I am a recent M.B.A. graduate of the University of Wisconsin at Madison. My area of concentration was Accounting; please see the attached resume for a list of relevant courses. I feel that my studies have prepared me for a position at Parker Thomas.

Prior to my graduate degree, I earned a B.A. in Accounting from the University of Chicago. While there, I won the Leopold Scholarship, which is given to an outstanding senior by the Accounting Department.

The enclosed resume provides further details about my preparation for an accounting career. I would also welcome the opportunity to present my qualifications in person and to learn more about your current needs in the area of accounting. I will call early next week regarding possible job openings. Thank you for your time and consideration.

Sincerely,

William Gavin

December 13, 20--

Hollywood Reporter
Box 1140-H
465 Hollywood Way
Burbank, CA 91505

I am responding to your ad in last week's edition for a public relations assistant at a major Hollywood production company. I am enclosing my resume and salary requirements as requested.

I am a recent graduate of California State University at Northridge, where I received a B.A. in Communications. My work includes an internship at Warner Bros. Studios in Burbank in the public relations department. I acquired many skills during this internship that will contribute to a career in public relations in the entertainment industry.

I am eager to learn more about this position and look forward to hearing from you soon. Please feel free to call me at the phone numbers listed below. Thank you for your time and consideration.

Sincerely,

Ken Phillips
4000 Sunset Blvd.
Los Angeles, CA 90028
K.Phillips@xxx.com
213/555-7648 (Home)
213/555-2000 (Work)

TYRELL STEVENSON   602 South Texas Avenue • Oakland, CA 94608
t.stevenson@xxx.com • (415) 555-3168

February 18, 20--

Richard Spiro
Manager, Seattle Hilton Hotel
1131 6th Street
Seattle, WA 98802

Mr. Spiro:

I am looking to enter into the hotel business with a long-term goal of management. I am forwarding my resume to you with the hope that you may have an opening on your staff.

I recently received a Certificate in Hotel Management from the International School of Business in San Francisco. I also completed an internship at the Eastmont Hotel, assisting the Food and Beverage Manager with all aspects of the business.

My previous work experience includes management of my own cookware business and employment as a travel consultant. In each of these positions my supervisors and business associates have praised me for being reliable, hard working, and competent. I feel that these positions have also helped me fine-tune my management, customer service, and computer skills.

Thank you for taking the time to review my qualifications. I am available at your convenience if you wish to schedule an interview.

Sincerely,

Tyrell Stevenson

Jennifer Wayans
4500 77th Street
New York, NY 10032
J.Wayans@xxx.com
(212) 555-3839

August 28, 20--

George Jacobs
Human Resources
AT&T
1200 5th Avenue
New York, NY 10019

Dear Mr. Jacobs:

Mitchell Sanderson, who works in the sales department at AT&T, suggested that I contact you regarding a possible opening in your public relations department. I have enclosed my resume for your consideration.

I will be graduating this month from New York University with a degree in Communications and an emphasis in Public Relations. I was recently inducted into the Communications Honor Society (Beta Alpha Psi), and I am also a member of the Association of International Business (A.I.B.). I feel that my education has prepared me for a successful career in the communications industry, and I would like to begin by putting my skills to use at AT&T.

I look forward to speaking with you further about opportunities within AT&T, and I will follow up next week with a call to your office. Thank you in advance for your time and consideration.

Sincerely,

Jennifer Wayans

April 7, 20--

Helena Borgess
Director of Human Resources
Warner Bros., Inc.
4000 Olive Avenue
Burbank, CA 91505

Dear Ms. Borgess:

I am writing to inquire about openings in your company in the area of Human Resources. I am interested in working in the entertainment industry while utilizing my personnel skills.

I will be graduating from UCLA with a degree in Business in June of this year. During my schooling, my focus has been primarily on Human Resources. Last summer, I served as an intern in the Human Resources department at TPT Inc., where I assisted with personnel acquisition and evaluation. During my time at TPT, I was able to put my education to practical use doing such things as administering tests to prospective employees and setting up appointments for interviews.

The enclosed resume provides further details regarding my experience. My contact information is listed below; please feel free to contact me if you would like to speak further regarding my qualifications.

Sincerely,

Reva Mendoza
University of California—Los Angeles
144 Glendon Avenue
Los Angeles, CA 90289
R.Mendoza@xxx.com
213-555-2384

Travis Shavers

15 E. Greenview St., Apt. 333
Richmond, VA 23229
T.Shavers@xxx.com
804-555-3903

May 12, 20--

Wendell C. Wilkerson
Editor
Richmond Register
330 S. Potomac Dr.
Richmond, VA 23238

Dear Mr. Wilkerson:

I am writing in response to your opening for a beat reporter that was posted at the University of Virginia. I am currently seeking a position in the field of journalism and wish to be considered for this opening.

I will graduate this June with a B.A. in Journalism from the University of Virginia. My writing and reporting experience includes positions as the Senior Editor of the campus newspaper, as an editor for a literary magazine, and as a broadcast journalism intern with WRCH-TV, all right here in Richmond.

I have enclosed my resume as well as writing samples for your review. I think you will find that my skills and background have prepared me for a position at the *Richmond Register*. I would like to discuss this position further; please feel free to contact me at your convenience for an interview. Thank you for your consideration.

Sincerely,

Travis Shavers

MARTIN C. CHAN

64 Collin Road • Miami, FL 33109 • martin.chan@xxx.com • 305-555-7757

September 9, 20--

Peter Donaghy
Managing Director
Donaghy Productions, Inc.
550 Magnolia Way
Burbank, CA 91501

Dear Mr. Donaghy:

Are you in need of a dedicated, energetic, resourceful production assistant?

After receiving my B.A. in Film Production in 2003, I have spent the last year working in Miami for New Order Productions as a production assistant. I also served as production coordinator for Tert Film Productions in Chicago and was the production assistant for the Baltimore Film Festival. I have benefited greatly from this experience, but it has always been my dream to work in the Hollywood film industry.

I would like to apply the skills and experience I have acquired to a position within Donaghy Productions. I feel that I could contribute to your company's quality work and be a productive new member of your staff. I hope the enclosed resume interests you. I will follow this letter with a phone call next week to discuss positions you may have available.

Sincerely,

Martin C. Chan

Terrence Wallace

700 Thornborough Road
Chattanooga, TN 37415
Terry.Wallace@xxx.com
615-555-2111

May 17, 20--

David D. Vargas
Director of Broadcast Operations
WGN-TV
2501 West Bradley Place
Chicago, IL 60618

Mr. Vargas:

I enjoyed meeting with you at the Broadcast Careers Seminar at Howard University last spring. I am writing to you now to express my interest in an opening at WGN for a News Assistant. I have enclosed my resume for your review.

In addition to my Journalism degree, I have gained experience over the last four summers in a variety of workplaces. Most recently, I completed an internship at WDC-TV in Washington, DC, where I assisted in the production of a news show. Previous internships include *Capitol Magazine*, *Chattanooga News*, and Park Advertising, Inc. During my internships, I was able to put my education to use and gain valuable experience and skills.

I will be graduating next month and I would be glad to come to Chicago for an interview at your convenience. Thank you for your time and consideration.

Sincerely,

Terrence Wallace

April 23, 20--

Sarah Eunsook
Director
Santa Barbara Art Fair
6660 Forest Green Avenue
Santa Barbara, CA 93299

Dear Ms. Eunsook:

I recently viewed the posting for a photographer for this year's Santa Barbara Art Fair, and I am interested in applying for the position.

My photography experience includes serving as the official photographer for the Nevada State Fair last year, where I headed a team of eight photographers. I have worked with digital, 35mm, and medium-format cameras along with video equipment. My photos have been used for a variety of products, including promotions, press releases, and publications.

I am a graduate of the University of Washington in Tacoma, where I earned a degree in Graphic Arts with a minor in Photography. I also have extensive experience as a graphic designer and often incorporate my photography into marketing and sales materials.

My resume is enclosed, along with some samples of my photography. You may also visit my website at www.****.com for a more extensive look at my work. As you will see, my background has prepared me for this job, and I would appreciate the opportunity to speak with you about it further. Please feel free to contact me at the phone number or e-mail address listed below. Thank you for your consideration.

Sincerely,

Peter Klept
554 Grambling Road
Santa Barbara, CA 93770
Klept-Photography@xxx.com
(805) 555-2332

Janis Darien

345 West 3rd Street, Apt. 42

Boston, MA 02210

j.darien@xxx.com

(617) 555-3291

July 23, 20--

David Bass
Sears & Roebuck, Inc.
1000 West Adams Street
Chicago, IL 60601

Mr. Bass:

I am responding to your job listing for a Marketing Management Trainee, which was posted in the placement office at Boston University. I am interested in applying for this position and have enclosed my resume with this letter.

I have recently graduated from Boston University with a degree in Economics, and I am eager to find employment in the marketing field. My work experience includes employment as a Marketing Assistant for Lewis Advertising Agency and as a Telephone Interviewer for Paterno Marketing, both in Boston. I believe that my skills and experience would be a perfect fit with the Sears trainee position, and I would like to have an opportunity to speak with you in person. I would be willing to relocate for such a position.

I will be in the Chicago area the week of August 12. Would it be possible to set up an interview with you during that week? If so, please contact me at your earliest convenience.

Sincerely,

Janis Darien

Clarence Smith

600 West Porter Street
Las Vegas, NV 89890
Clarence.Smith@xxx.com
(702) 555-3893

May 15, 20--

Mr. Tarskett Renu
Creative Director
Quest Advertising
2330 West Delaney Boulevard
Los Angeles, CA 90029

Dear Mr. Renu:

This is a letter of inquiry. I am curious to know whether there are any openings in your agency at the present time.

I expect to graduate next month from the University of Nevada with a B.A. in Communications, and I am looking toward a career in advertising. While at Nevada, I was awarded the Dornburn Academic Merit Scholarship and the Excellence in Communications Award. I also made the Dean's List four times.

Last summer, I gained experience in the field by serving as an advertising intern for Port Rand & Associates. There I assisted the sales staff in the areas of research, demographics, sales forecasts, and special promotions. The experience I gained in this internship, along with my education, has given me a good foundation for a career in advertising.

I have attached my resume for your review. I would appreciate hearing of any current openings at Quest, and I am willing to travel to Los Angeles at your convenience to discuss opportunities in person. Thank you for your consideration.

Sincerely,

Clarence Smith

THEODORE L. MCDONALD

2107 Adams Street, Apt. 9
Austin, TX 78711
t.mcdonald@xxx.com
(512) 555-7665

December 8, 20--

Melissa Ward
Human Resources
Austin Hospital
444 East Grand Avenue
Austin, TX 78712

Dear Ms. Ward:

This letter is in response to your ad in the *Austin Times* for a Dietitian for the children's wing of your hospital. I am enclosing my resume for your consideration in light of this opening.

The position interests me both because it matches my qualifications and because I have worked for Austin Hospital in the past as a volunteer. I gained valuable experience during two summers assisting your Head Dietitian with menus and meal planning. My first full-time job, as Assistant Nutritionist at the University of Texas, has been a challenge. I've helped to plan over 250 menus as well as oversee the interviewing and hiring of student workers. I have gained immeasurable skills from my position at the University of Texas and would like to bring my experience and enthusiasm to Austin Hospital.

I am a recent graduate of the University of Texas, where I received a B.S. in Nutrition. While at the university, I received the Spielberg Nutrition Award and earned a spot on the Dean's List four semesters.

The current opening at Austin Hospital sounds like a challenging one, and I feel that I am up to the challenge. I look forward to hearing from you regarding this opportunity.

Sincerely,

Theodore L. McDonald

CHRISTINE HARDING

3333 North Halen Avenue, Apt. 3B
Toronto, ONT M6P 4C7
E-mail: c.harding@xxx.com
Home: 416-555-2333

May 24, 20--

John D. Peck
Peck, Sylbert & Peck
55 East Monroe Street
Toronto, ONT M6P 4C7

Dear Mr. Peck:

Professor Gerald Stevens at the Toronto School of Law suggested that I write to you to inquire about an opening at your law firm. I will be graduating from the Toronto School next month with a Juris Doctor degree and a concentration in Health-care Litigation. It is my desire to remain in the Toronto area after graduation, and Professor Stevens highly recommends your firm.

Currently, I am interning at Tannen & Hope here in Toronto, where I draft legal documents, assist in trial preparation, and conduct legal research. This internship has been a valuable experience for me and has helped to prepare me for a career as an attorney.

My resume is enclosed for your review. I appreciate your consideration and will contact you next week regarding an interview.

Sincerely,

Christine Harding